Swimming Drills for Every Stroke

Human Kinetics

Library of Congress Cataloging-in-Publication Data

Guzman, Ruben J., 1957-
    Swimming drills for every stroke / Ruben J. Guzman.
        p.   cm.
    ISBN: 0-88011-769-9
    1. Swimming--Study and teaching.   I. Title.
GV836.35.G89   1998
797.2'1--dc21   97-42343
                                                             CIP

ISBN: 0-88011-769-9

Acquisitions Editor: Ken Mange; **Developmental Editor:** Kristine Enderle; **Assistant Editor:** Laura Hambly; **Editorial Assistant:** Laura Ward Majersky; **Copyeditor:** Jackie Blakley; **Proofreader:** Erin Cler; **Graphic Designer:** Stuart Cartwright; **Graphic Artist:** Denise Lowry; **Photo Editor:** Boyd LaFoon; **Cover Designer:** Jack Davis; **Photographer (cover):** © the Stock Market/Pete Saloutos; **Illustrator:** Roberto Sabas; **Printer:** Versa Press

Human Kinetics books are available at special discounts for bulk purchase. Special editions or book excerpts can also be created to specification. For details, contact the Special Sales Manager at Human Kinetics.

Printed in the United States of America   10   9   8   7   6   5   4   3

Human Kinetics
Web site: http://www.humankinetics.com/

United States: Human Kinetics, P.O. Box 5076, Champaign, IL 61825-5076
1-800-747-4457
e-mail: humank@hkusa.com

Canada: Human Kinetics, 475 Devonshire Road, Unit 100, Windsor, ON N8Y 2L5
1-800-465-7301 (in Canada only)
e-mail: humank@hkcanada.com

Europe: Human Kinetics, P.O. Box IW14, Leeds LS16 6TR, United Kingdom
+44 (0)113-278 1708
e-mail: humank@hkeurope.com

Australia: Human Kinetics, 57A Price Avenue, Lower Mitcham, South Australia 5062
(08) 82771555
e-mail: liahka@senet.com.au

New Zealand: Human Kinetics, P.O. Box 105-231, Auckland Central
09-523-3462
e-mail: humank@hknewz.com

CONTENTS

INTRODUCTION

Swimming requires a combination of physical strength and technical finesse. Because the water is a foreign land to humans, the technical aspects of moving through the water become much more critical at the competitive level. Most swimmers participating in the sport are relatively inexperienced in proper technique. For them, progress is most dramatic when their technique improves. But for even the most experienced swimmers, small technical improvements can make the difference between qualifying for nationals and not qualifying.

As a swimmer, I was fortunate to have been taught by Owen Hahn, the great swimming and football coach for Bell High School in Southeast Los Angeles. Coach Hahn was a master of teaching fundamentals whose methods enhanced his athletes' ability to swim faster. I became a decent swimmer who learned how to effectively use technical skills to outperform more talented swimmers. As a coach, I was influenced by the systematic teaching approach of John Wooden, the great basketball coach at UCLA. The result is a curriculum I have developed, refined, used, and tested for over 15 years. In the process, many of my swimmers have greatly improved their technical skills and performances.

This book covers the fundamentals needed for competitive swimming. All of the essential drills are presented to assure that a swimmer is competent in the basics of competitive swimming. Mastering the basics provides the foundation for future development and refinement.

Swimmers need to have a planned approach to developing good technique that is simple to learn, and successfully proven and tested. Swimmers who use this book will benefit by learning effective ways to practice the skills of swimming. They will perform better and swim faster in competition. They are more likely to stay interested in swimming and will therefore enjoy the sport more.

Coaches need to have a well-planned, comprehensive curriculum. They also need a system that is flexible and can be adapted to a variety of situations. This book will benefit coaches by providing an organized approach to stroke instruction. By using this system, they can communicate the course outline more effectively in advance, thereby gaining support from the swimmers and parents. Once a coach becomes skilled in using these drills, he or she can easily detect and correct stroke deficiencies, allowing the athletes to become faster and better swimmers.

HOW TO USE THIS BOOK

Let's say you have sixteen weeks to prepare for a major competition. A good way to organize instruction is to divide drill training into three sections. Spend the first nine weeks teaching the drills presented in this book in sequential order. Cover one chapter a week. Next, repeat the drills in chapters 3-6 to polish and correct technique. This lasts four weeks. To wrap up, spend three weeks focusing on starts, turns, and finishes (chapters 7-9), along with brushing up any major stroke deficiencies.

Once you have your overall 16-week plan in place, organize each week like this:

- Day 1: Introduce the first two or three drills.
- Day 2: Review drills learned on Day 1, and then introduce two or three new drills.
- Day 3: Review all previously learned drills. Next teach the final set of drills.
- Days 4 and 5: Review all key drills in sequence.

Do your normal warm-up routine, but include at least one key drill learned the previous day. Once the entire system has been covered, a key drill from each stroke also becomes part of the warm-up. Each week, change the key drill. Key drills should be memorized by your swimmers and performed weekly.

To introduce and teach each drill, follow these steps:

- **Explain.** Provide a complete description of how the drill is performed.
- **Demonstrate.** Show how the drill is performed by using the diagrams, or demonstrate the drill yourself.
- **Correct.** Have swimmers perform the drill after your initial explanation and demonstration. Point out what is done correctly. Next, focus on one point at a time. Correct any errors until the drill is done properly.
- **Repeat.** Once the swimmers perform the drill correctly, repeat it until the drill becomes a habit. Make sure the swimmers do not develop improper techniques.

To coaches, your job is not an easy one and the rewards come all too slowly. I hope this material makes your job easier and more enjoyable.

To swimmers, my hope is that you enjoy performing these drills. There is so much to learn about swimming. Just learn it a little at a time. I hope this book helps you master all of the important skills and helps you swim easier and faster.

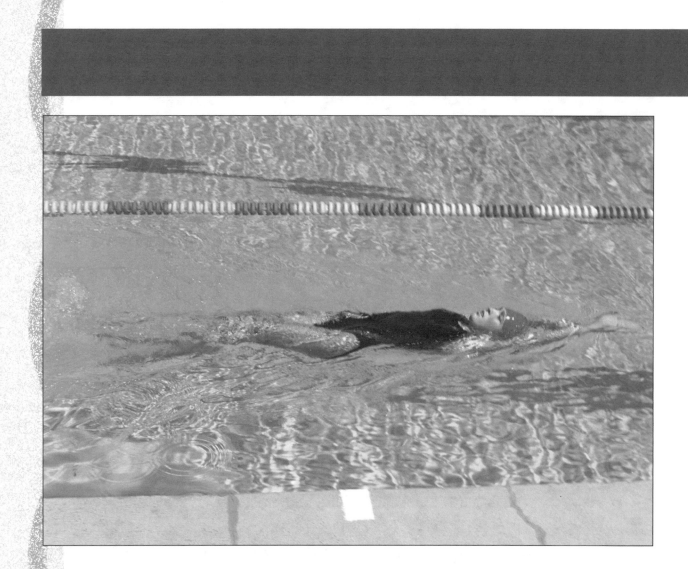

CHAPTER ONE

Breathing and Kicking

The proper mechanics of breathing and kicking might be the simplest skills to perform in swimming. Yet these skills are often overlooked. Proper breathing and kicking are critical for the swimmer to feel comfortable in the water, have good body position, and move through the water quickly and efficiently.

Fast and efficient swimmers

- slice through the water with their body in a streamline position—if they swim with less drag and less friction in the water, they save energy and time; and

- breathe comfortably and relaxed—if they hold their breath, they waste energy.

The drills in this chapter will help swimmers do just that—swim in a streamline position and learn proper breathing. Correction of breathing or body position can often lead to dramatic results. This chapter is the foundation for excellent swimming technique.

1

Over and Under Breathing

Purpose

To ensure correct breathing. Breathing should flow in a relaxed manner—holding your breath wastes energy.

Description

1. Hold on to the gutter with both hands, facing the wall. Feet are positioned against the wall or on the bottom.
2. Move your head up and down from just above the surface of the water to just below the surface.
3. As soon as your mouth and nose go below the surface, breathe out and blow steady bubbles. Breathe in only when your mouth is above the surface.
4. Breathe slowly and stay relaxed. Repeat the motion at least 20 times in a row.

Focus Point

Do not continue to breathe out when you lift your head up. If someone can hear you breathing out, or if you spray water out of your mouth, then you need to concentrate on breathing out only underwater, and breathing in only above water.

Tip

- Place a candle (real or imaginary) in front of you above the surface. Don't blow out the candle!

a.

b.

Flutter Kick Deck Drill

Purpose

To help swimmers see and feel how to do the flutter kick.

Description

1. Sit on the edge of the deck. With your toes pointed and legs extended straight over the water, touch just your toes to the surface of the water. Lower your legs so that your feet are about 12 inches under the water. Keep your legs close together.

2. Slowly raise one foot toward the surface, then lower it back 12 inches under the water while raising the other foot. Continue alternately raising and lowering your feet, making sure the feet are close together as they pass each other. Keep the toes pointed toward the opposite end of the pool.

3. Kick the water up toward the surface, but do not go above the surface. Gradually increase the speed of the kick.

4. As the speed increases, gradually bend your knees just a little and relax the ankles.

Focus Points

- Keep your toes pointed toward the opposite end of the pool. Avoid pointing the toes up to the sky.

- "Boil" the water, but do not splash. Kick under the water, not in the air.

Tips

- Ask someone to stand in the water and hold his hand just under the water with his palm facing the pool floor. Kick the palm flat with the top of your foot. If your toes hit first, they need to be pointed more.

- Practice leg raises. Holding on to a bar or the back of a chair, stand straight with one foot flat on the ground. With the other leg, point the toes and touch the big toe to the ground. Keep your leg straight. Then slowly lift the leg up about 12 inches off the ground and hold for two seconds. Slowly lower your leg and touch your toe to the ground. Repeat 10 to 20 times. Switch legs.

2

Push and Float

Purpose

To practice the proper body position for the backstroke.

Description

1. Hold on to the gutter or wall and place your feet on the wall at around hip depth.

2. Let go of the wall and slowly push off using your legs. Straighten your body and float along the surface for about five seconds.

3. Keep your arms at your sides. Arch your back a little so that your abdomen stays up along the surface. It's OK if your legs sink a little.

4. Breathe comfortably and keep your upper body on the surface.

Focus Points

- Be sure to keep your head back far enough so that your ears are just under the water.

- Point your toes as you float.

Tip

Ask someone to place a half-board on your abdomen as you begin to float. See how long you can keep it there.

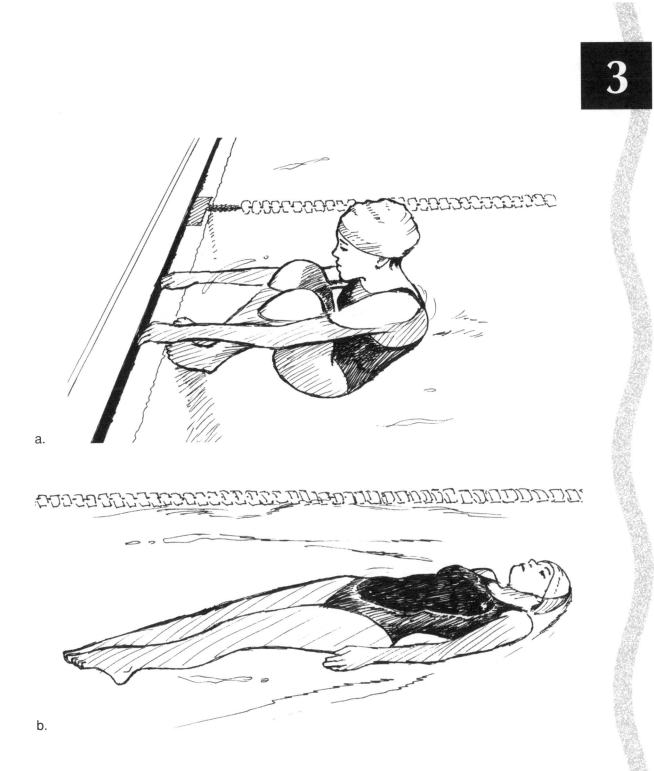

a.

b.

4

Slow Flutter

Purpose

To practice correct body position for the backstroke while adding a kicking action.

Description

1. Begin with the floating position as in the previous drill, and gradually add a slow flutter kick. Kick just fast enough to keep your body on the surface.
2. Kick about half a lap and then stop.
3. Turn around and repeat the kicking exercise. Be careful to stop before you get to the wall on the return trip.

Focus Points

- Kick as slowly as possible while maintaining the correct body position.
- Stay relaxed! Keep your head back and enjoy.

Tip

You can use the half-board technique as described in the previous drill.

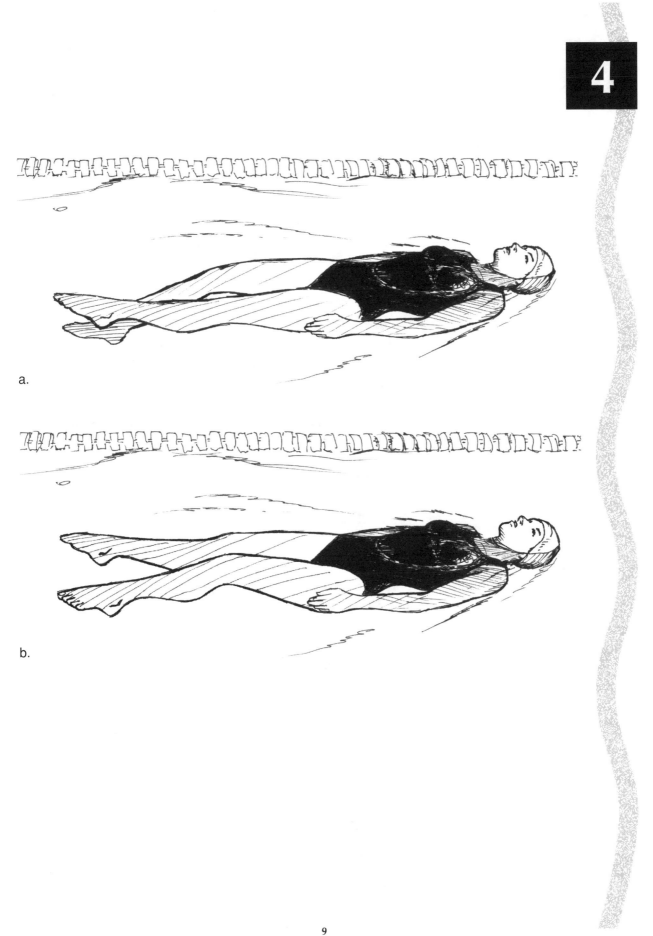

a.

b.

5

Streamline Kicking

Purpose

To introduce the streamline arm position with kicking. A good streamline will reduce friction and help you slice through the water with very little energy.

Description

1. Place one hand over the other with your fingers together. It does not matter which hand goes on top.

2. Wrap the thumb of the hand on top around the lower hand to "lock" your hands so that you cannot pull them apart.

3. Straighten your arms overhead so that you squeeze your head between your arms. Your arms should be at least slightly behind your ears.

4. Push off the wall to a floating position as in Drill 3 (Push and Float), but hold a streamline position.

5. Gradually add a slow kick while keeping your abdomen up. Think in the following pattern: *float, streamline, kick.*

Focus Points

- Concentrate on each aspect in the order of the key words: *float, streamline, kick.*

- Relax. Don't force it.

- Keep your toes pointed and your ankles relaxed. Kick slowly. Keep your head back.

- Keep your hands just under the water.

Tips

- The kickboard technique described in Drill 3 (Push and Float) works well here.

- Stand in front of a mirror to check your streamline position.

- There are three rules for an excellent streamline. Commit these to memory!

  1. One hand over the other.

  2. Lock the thumb.

  3. Squeeze the head.

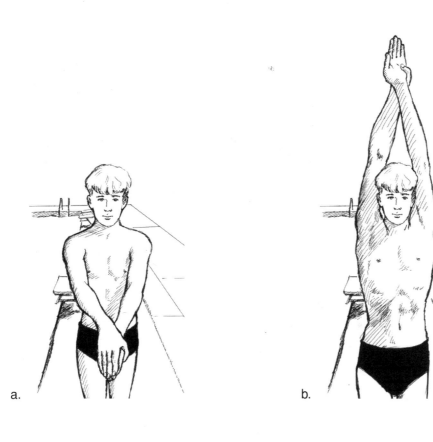

a.

b.

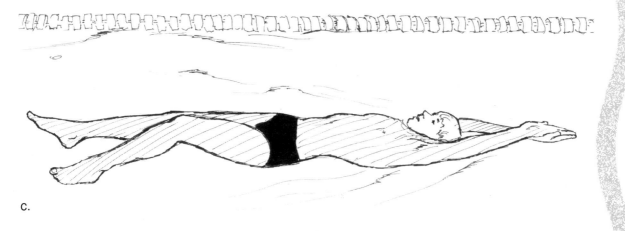

c.

6

Backstroke Kick

Purpose

To practice full-speed backstroke kicking while maintaining correct body position.

Description

1. Put fins on. Repeat the previous drill, holding a good streamline and correct body position.
2. Begin to kick more forcefully and quickly.

Focus Points

- Remember: *float, streamline, kick.*
- Keep your hands just under the water.
- Keep toes pointed and ankles relaxed.
- Boil the water, but do not splash.
- Keep your head back so that your ears are just barely under the water.
- Keep your abdomen up.

Tip

See how hard you can kick so as to boil the water as much as possible. Have a boiling contest with a friend!

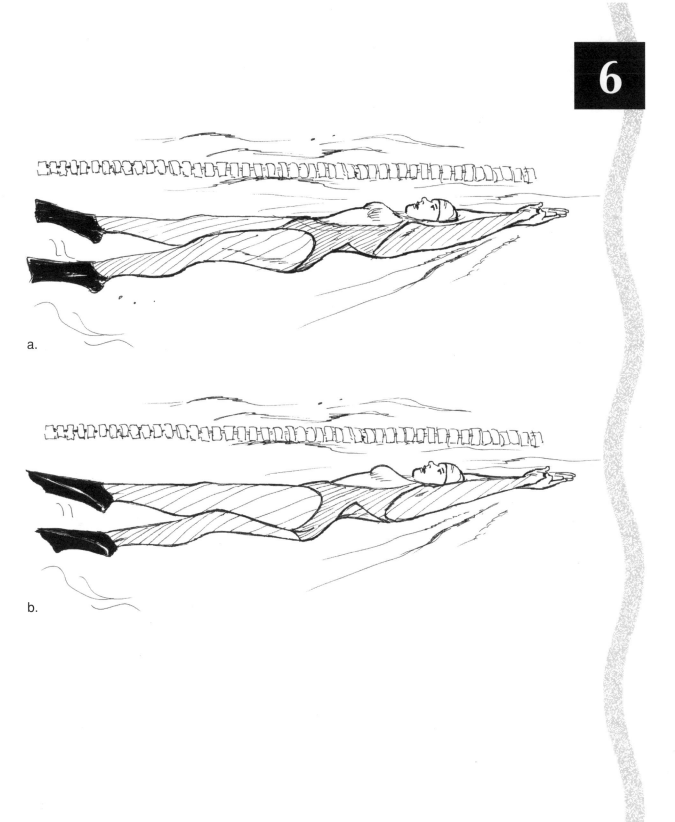

a.

b.

7

Lateral Kick

Purpose

To establish good kicking mechanics for the lateral kick, which is used in the freestyle and backstroke.

Description

1. Wear fins. Start at the wall. Hold a half-board with one arm so that your forearm rests on the surface of the board and the fingers wrap around the top.

2. Push off from the wall and place your other arm down at your side.

3. Roll your body at the shoulder of the arm holding the board so that your opposite shoulder is well above the surface of the water and your torso and hips are perpendicular to the surface of the water.

4. Begin kicking with a quick flutter kick. Rest your head comfortably on the surface of the water so that your ear is just under the water and the edge of your eye is at the surface. The corner of your mouth will be just under the surface. Alternate sides after each lap.

Focus Points

• Keep your body position steady.

• Keep your feet kicking quickly, with very little knee bend.

Tip

If you wear Zoomers, try to feel the kicking in both directions. ("Zoomers" is a special brand of swim fins used by competitive swimmers. The fins are designed to help swimmers develop kicking force in both directions.)

a.

b.

8

Freestyle Kick

Purpose

To develop good kicking mechanics while kicking freestyle on your front side. This position is frequently used in training sets.

Description

1. Wear fins. Start at the wall. Use a half-board.
2. Push off the wall and place both hands on the half-board, keeping the arms straight.
3. Begin kicking with a quick flutter kick. Keep your toes in the water at all times. The heels of your feet should just barely break the surface of the water. Your hips should be right at the surface.
4. Look straight ahead. Lower your face into the water to breathe out. Lift your chin to the surface to breathe in.

Focus Points

- Keep your arms straight.
- Kick the water, not the air. In other words, avoid lifting your feet above the surface of the water.
- Keep your hips up.
- Make sure your breathing is relaxed.

Tip

When lowering your face into the water, try to position your eyes just below the surface. This will help get you ready for the freestyle drills.

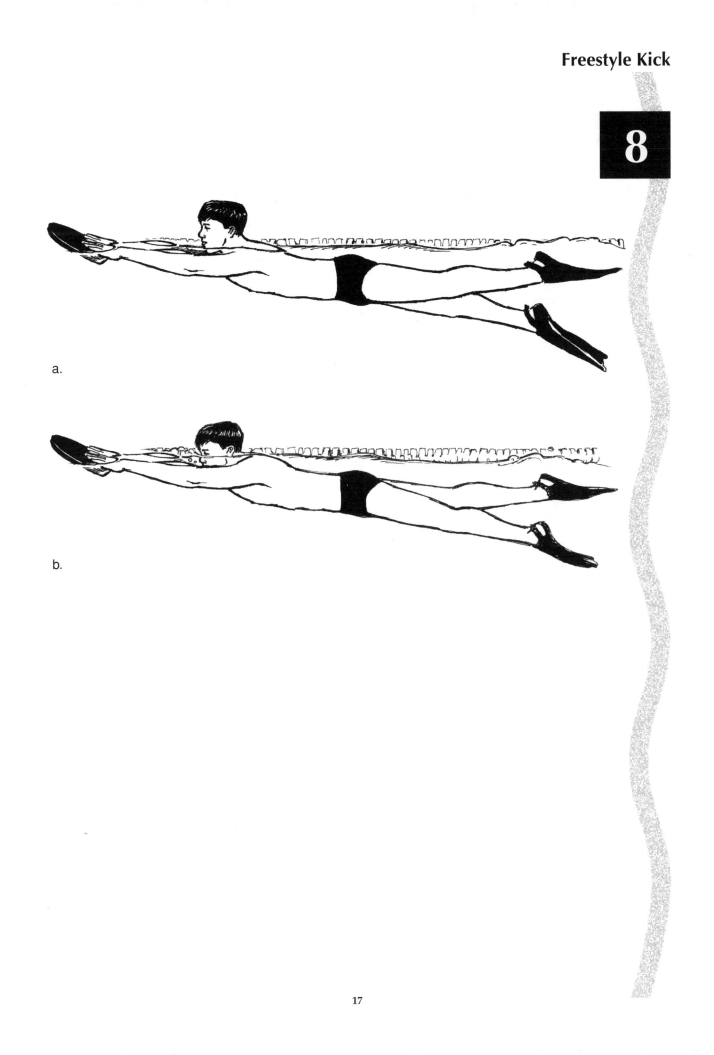

a.

b.

Breaststroke Kick Deck Drill

Purpose

To help swimmers see and feel how a proper breaststroke kick is done.

Description

1. Sit on the edge of the deck with your legs extended over the water. Keep your heels just below the surface at all times during this exercise. Begin with your legs together and toes pointed, with the inner sides of your feet touching.

2. Bring the legs *in* toward your body (flex at the knees and draw your thighs upward) so the knees are about shoulder-width apart, the heels are close together, and the toes point to the sides of the pool.

3. Rotate your feet *out* to catch the water with the inner sides of the feet, keeping the knees about shoulder-width apart.

4. Begin to *squeeze* the water between your legs while keeping your feet flexed.

5. Bring your legs completely *together* and finish with your toes pointed. You should see and feel a powerful squeeze of the water.

Focus Points

- Develop the following pattern: *in, out, squeeze, together.*
- Be sure to finish each kick with the knees straight and the toes pointed.
- Catch as much water as possible on the sides of your feet when you squeeze your legs together.

Tips

- You can practice this kick almost anywhere. Try it while sitting down on the floor watching television. Or you can sit on your bed and practice it before you go to sleep.
- For an advanced version, begin in a leg lift position and do not let the feet touch. This variation is great for the abdominals!

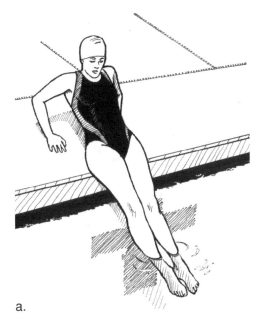

a.

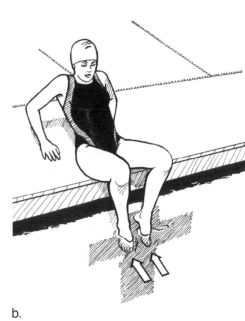

b.

c.

d.

10

Inverted Breaststroke Kick

Purpose

To develop a balanced breaststroke kick with good body control. This drill helps to prevent exaggerated hip action and improper leg mechanics. Anyone with a weak breaststroke kick should emphasize this drill.

Description

1. Start by pushing off the wall to float on your back into a streamline position along the surface. Be sure to float!

2. After counting to three (one thousand one, one thousand two, one thousand three), begin and complete a breaststroke kick.

3. Count to three between each repetition.

Focus Points

- Keep your upper-body position stable. Your head should not go under the water. If it does, it usually means you are not keeping your feet up high enough.

- Keep a tight streamline. Your hands should stay just below the surface.

- Finish each kick with the body in a floating position, and the toes pointed and near the surface.

- Do not allow your knees to rise more than 1 inch above the surface.

Tip

Move across the pool with as few kicks as possible. Make it a contest with a friend!

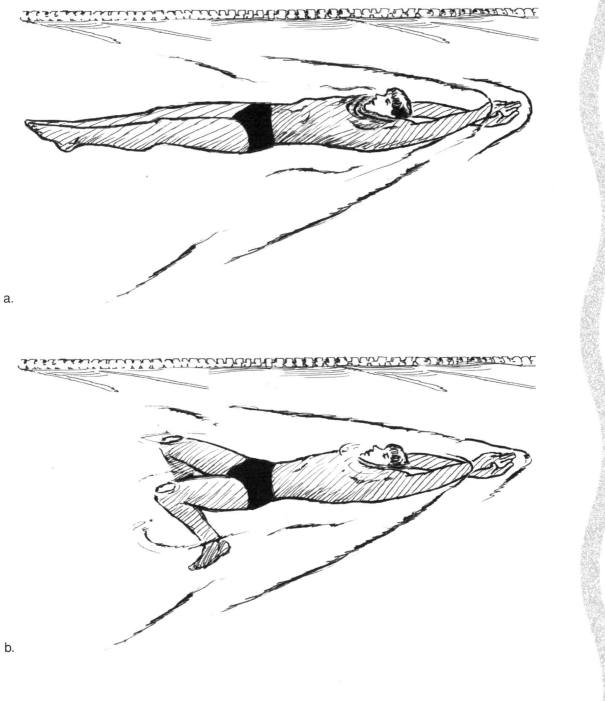

a.

b.

11

Head-Up Breaststroke Kick

Purpose

To progress in the development of the breaststroke kick.

Description

1. Hold a half-board at the sides with your thumbs on top. Keep your head up so that your chin is on the surface of the water and you can breathe comfortably.
2. Push off the pool wall with your arms straight. As in the previous drill, count to three and then begin and complete a breaststroke kick. Be sure to float your body as high as you can!
3. Count to three between each repetition.

Focus Points

- Keep your hips right at the surface at all times.
- Keep your arms straight.
- Finish each kick with a tight squeeze and toes pointed.
- Each time you keep your feet together for a count of three is called a *glide*—you'll need to remember this for later drills.
- Keep your knees from drifting wider than shoulder-width apart.

Tips

- Have someone watch to make sure you are squeezing the kick and keeping your hips up.
- Move across the pool with as few kicks as possible.

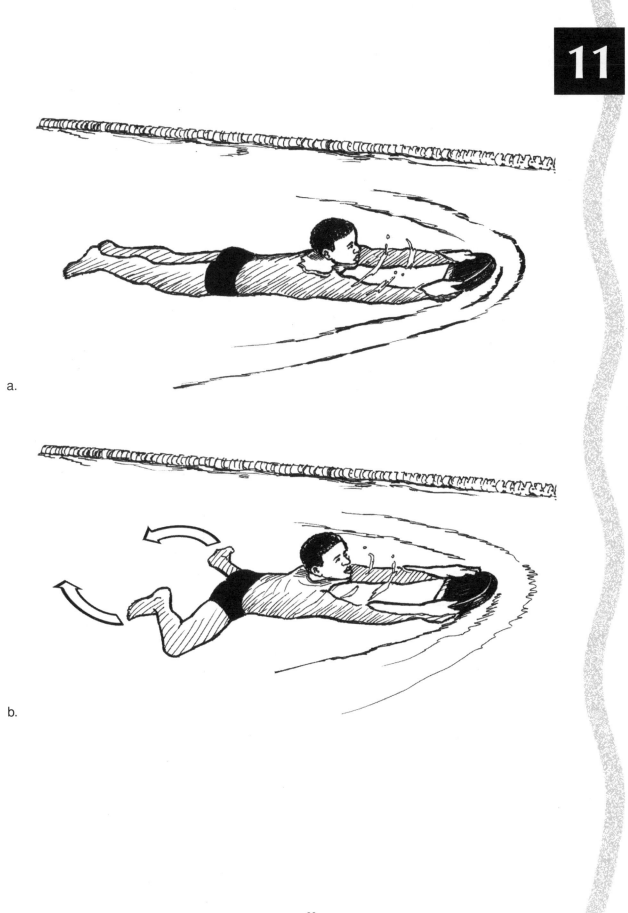

a.

b.

Breaststroke Breathe and Kick

Purpose

To coordinate the timing of breathing with kicking and gliding in the breaststroke.

Description

1. Hold a half-board at the sides with your thumbs on top. Start by pushing off from the pool wall with your face in the water so that your eyes are just below the water. You should be looking forward enough to barely see the half-board, but keep your chin tucked in.

2. Stretch into a glide position with your legs together, toes pointed, and hips up. Silently, count to three. Be sure to blow bubbles the whole time your face is in the water.

3. Lift your head up so that your chin is on the surface. *Breathe* in and begin your *kick* by bringing your legs in.

4. Then as you kick out and squeeze, lower your head and begin to breathe out. Complete the kick and hold the *glide* for a count of three, then repeat.

Focus Points

- Develop this pattern: *breathe, kick, glide.*
- After you finish the glide, lift your head.

Tip

Keep the chin tucked in when you breathe. This will be important to remember for other breaststroke drills as well.

12

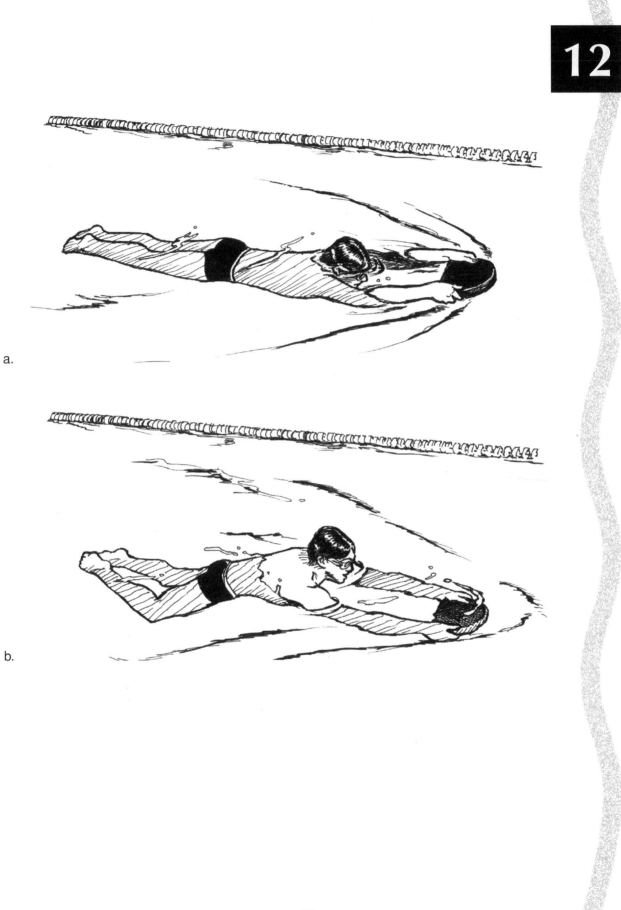

a.

b.

13

Butterfly Kick Deck Drill

Purpose

To feel the body action of the butterfly stroke.

Description

1. Stand on the deck with your hands on your hips. Be sure to keep good back posture at all times during this exercise—avoid rounding the back and shoulders. Always look forward.

2. Begin by pushing your hips back and your chest forward, while keeping your back and legs straight. (The correct position will feel a little like starting to lean over to get a drink of water from a drinking fountain.) Push your hips as far back as you can while still maintaining your balance.

3. Return your hips to a straight position. Then push your hips forward, bending your knees slightly and keeping your back slightly arched. Once again return to the straight position.

4. Once you are comfortable with the motions, start to blend them in a smooth continuous action. Try to feel your hips moving through a full range of motion.

Focus Points

- Be sure to keep your neck flexible so you always look forward. Your chin should be tucked in when your hips are forward and should stick out when your hips are back.

- Keep a slight arch in your low back at all times.

- At first, push the hips as far forward and back as possible. Then speed it up and move your hips just a few inches forward and a few inches back.

Tips

- Practice in front of the mirror at home so that you can see that you are always looking forward.

- Do this drill in shallow water (about waist high) and really feel how the water moves!

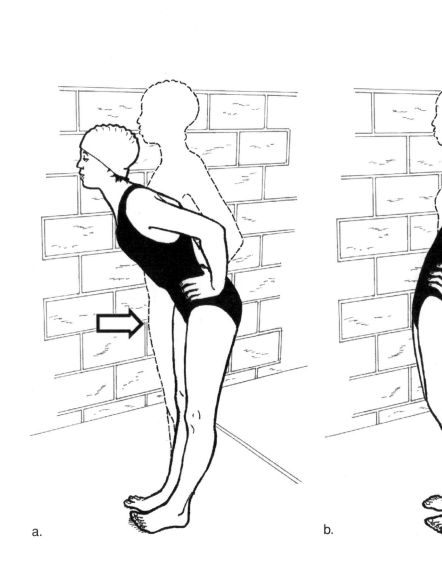

a.

b.

14

Inverted Dolphin Kick

Purpose

To practice the body action of the butterfly stroke.

Description

1. Wear fins. Push off the wall and float on your back with your arms down at your sides.

2. Begin the dolphin kick by pushing your abdominals up. Then progressively push your knees, and then your feet, up to the surface. This creates a whip action beginning with the abdominals. Your hands and head may go up and down a little; that's OK. Be sure to put one hand above your head to protect it as you approach the wall.

Focus Points

- Be sure to push the abdominals up above the surface on each kick.

- Bend your knees just a little and kick from the hips, not the knees.

Tips

- Start off underwater and then gradually come to the surface, and see if the kick feels the same.

- Do slow, big, powerful kicks at first. Build speed later.

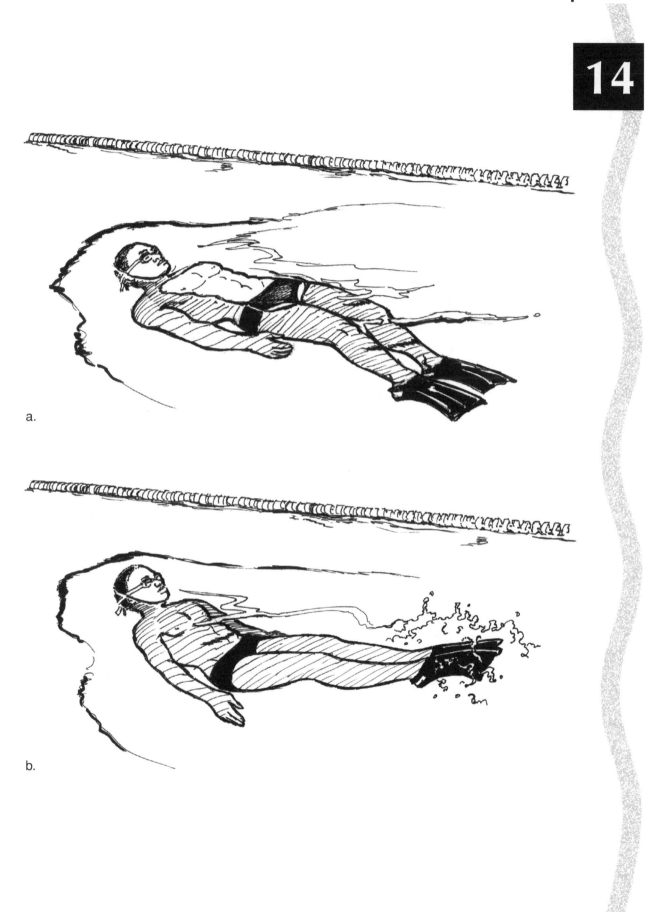

a.

b.

15

Streamline Inverted Dolphin Kick

Purpose

To practice the body action of the butterfly stroke.

Description

1. Use fins. Push off the wall and float on your back with your arms above your head in a streamline position.
2. Begin the dolphin kick by pushing your abdominals, then knees, and finally your feet, up to the surface.

Focus Points

- Be sure to push your abdominals up above the surface on each kick.
- Bend your knees just a little and kick from the hips, not the knees.

Tips

- Start off underwater and then gradually come to the surface, and see if the kick feels the same.
- Do slow, big, powerful kicks at first. Gradually build speed. As you get faster, the kicks will be shallower and quicker.

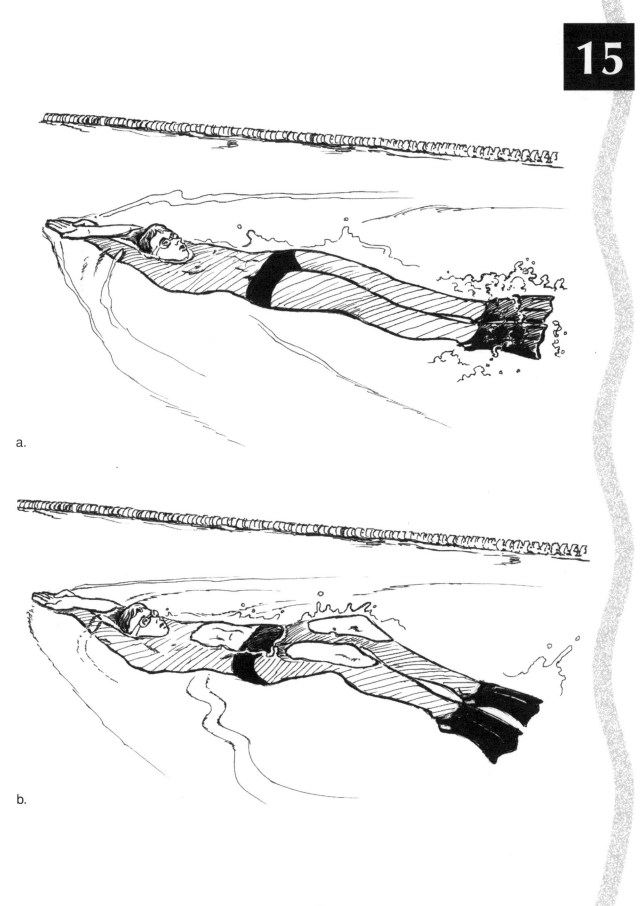

a.

b.

16

Dolphin Tail Walk

Purpose

To feel the body action, speed, and power of the butterfly kick.

Description

1. First, imagine watching the dolphins you would see at a marine park like Sea World. Picture the dolphins as they kick up above the surface and seem to walk backward on the surface with their tails. Their bodies move back and forth quickly and powerfully as they gradually move backward. This is what you will now attempt to imitate.

2. Use fins. Push off the wall on your back, with feet deep, arms down at your sides, and head above the surface. Use quick, strong dolphin kicks to keep your head and shoulders above the water as you gradually kick backward. This one is a challenge! You will really feel your abdominals!

Focus Points

- Feel the hips working back and forth as quickly and powerfully as possible.
- Bend your knees just a little and kick from the hips, not the knees.

Tips

- For an advanced version, keep your hands just above the surface at your sides.
- To build great power, try the drill while wearing a weight belt.

a.

b.

17

Underwater Dolphin Kick

Purpose

To feel the complete body action of the butterfly.

Description

1. Imagine yourself as a mermaid swimming along easily under the sea.

2. Use fins. Begin by pushing off the wall on your front side along the surface, keeping your hands down by your sides and looking down at the bottom of the pool. Do not use your arms at all on this drill.

3. Tuck your chin in and do a surface dive. You will go down first with your head, then your hips, and finally your "tail."

4. Just as your "tail" enters the water, do a strong dolphin kick. Go completely underwater and then level off to do as many dolphin kicks as you can before surfacing to breathe.

Focus Points

- Do the surface dive very slowly. Really feel your body slide into the deeper water.

- Be sure to keep your head moving at all times.

- Look down at the black line on the bottom of the pool. If you are looking forward, your hips will not be able to create enough power for a strong kick.

Tip

Have someone watch you under the water to see that you are not looking forward.

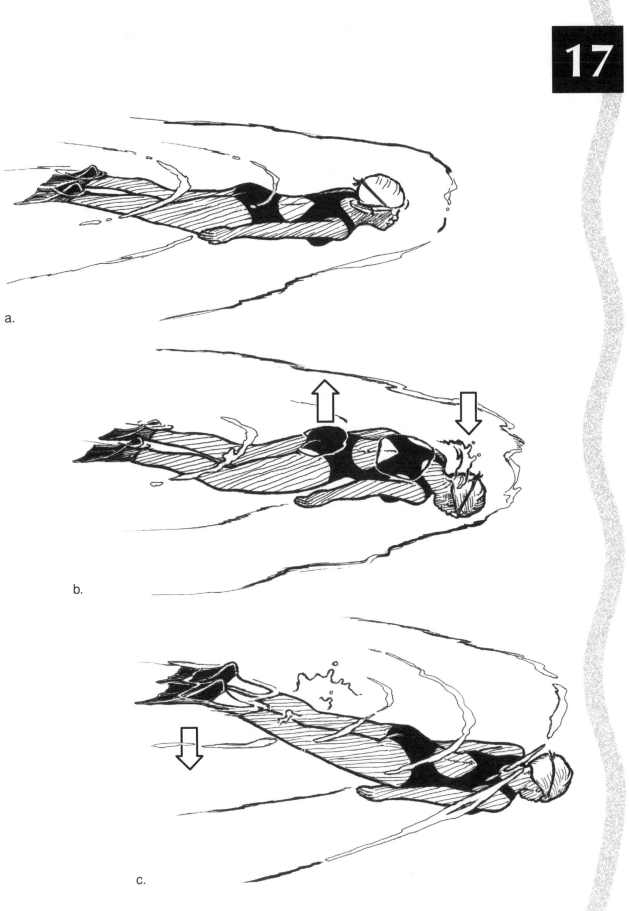

a.

b.

c.

CHAPTER TWO

Sculling

In order for the arm action of all the strokes to be effective, swimmers need to learn how to generate propulsion through the shape of their hands and forearms as they move through the water. Sculling drills may be the best way of learning the "propeller" propulsion methods of swimming that have long been described by swimming scientists as the most effective.

These drills are a practical way to

- learn about the pitch, lift, and the angles of attack;
- improve the feel for the water;
- strengthen hands, forearms, and wrists; and
- practice pulling action, lifting action, and the finish of all strokes.

By modifying the position of the body and the direction of the sculling, swimmers can feel how to apply pressure in the water and position their fingers, hands, wrists, and forearms for the most effective movement. These drills offer a basic beginning to the art of sculling.

18

Sweep In, Sweep Out

Purpose

To develop coordination in sculling with both hands and to improve feel for the water.

Description

1. Stand in water about mid-chest depth. Start with both arms extended in front of you about shoulder-width apart.

2. Place one forearm and hand under the surface, palm down. First scull with just the right hand, and then just the left. (Each hand should trace a large figure-8 on its side. Sweep up and out, then sweep down and in—this is the basic sculling action.)

3. Next scull with the hands moving in opposite directions at the same time. First sweep out with both hands, then sweep in with both hands.

4. Start slowly with wide sweeping motions and gradually move your hands more quickly with smaller motions.

Focus Points

- Quickly change the angle of the hands as you move them through the water.

- Keep your wrists strong.

- Rotate from the elbow.

- Feel the pressure on the hands and forearms.

Tips

- Practice sculling with different hand shapes: a fist, two fingers, fingers together, fingers spread, and fingers together with the thumb out.

- This drill presents a very basic sculling action. The drills that follow use this basic action in some fun and challenging positions.

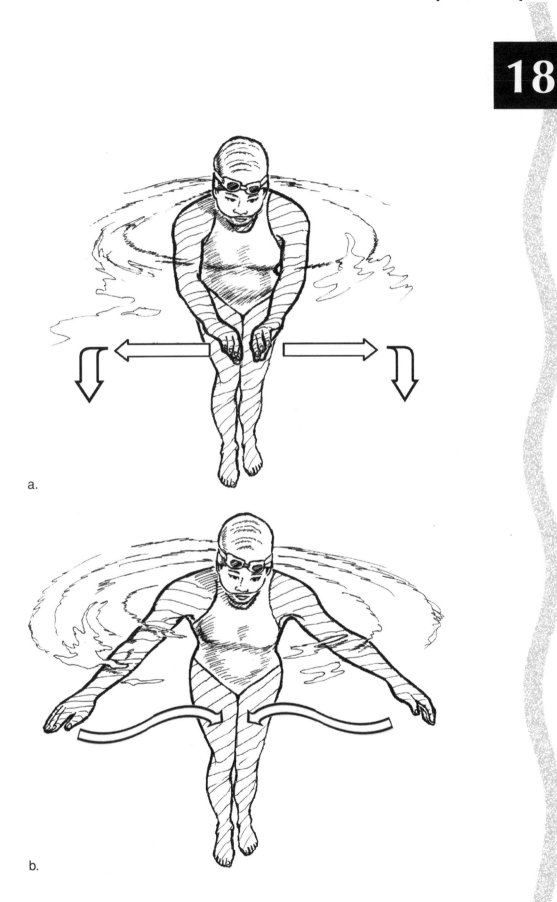

a.

b.

19

Deep-Water Scull

Purpose

To practice the sculling motion.

Description

1. Move to deeper water, where your feet cannot touch the bottom.

2. Practice the basic two-hand sculling action and keep your feet together. Be sure to keep your head up and your body straight.

3. Start by sculling just 20 seconds at a time, then try to gradually increase the amount of time to several minutes. It's a tough workout!

Focus Points

- Move your hands quickly.
- Keep your body straight.
- Keep your feet together.
- Keep your head up.

Tips

- For variety, change your body position very slowly while keeping the hand action very fast.
- Try any arm position, but don't kick.

a.

b.

20

Vertical Twists

Purpose

To practice body control while sculling.

Description

1. Start in deep water, so that your feet do not touch the bottom. Begin with the basic sculling action with both arms extended out at your sides.

2. While sculling with short, quick hand movements, and changing the angle of your hands, begin to rotate slowly in one direction for a couple of turns, and then reverse the direction.

3. Next, rotate with one hand behind your back, using short, quick hand movements. Alternate directions of rotation.

Focus Points

- Rotate slowly with short, quick hand movements.
- Keep your body straight.
- Keep your feet together.
- Keep your head up.

Tips

- If you have trouble staying up, try using a pull buoy between your legs.
- For an advanced variation, try doing this drill upside-down, with the feet above the surface.

a.

b.

21

Somersaults

Purpose

To feel the hands and forearms acting as "oars."

Description

1. Start in deep water so that your feet do not touch the bottom. (Preferably at least 6 feet deep.) Sink just under the water and tuck into a tight ball, keeping your chin tucked into your chest.

2. Extend your arms out to your sides. Keep the arms almost completely straight.

3. Begin to somersault forward, moving your arms quickly (sculling) in a circular motion.

4. If you are able, do two or three somersaults in a row.

5. Try doing reverse somersaults as well.

Focus Points

- Keep your arms extended.
- Keep your chin tucked in.
- Keep the sculling action of the hands short and quick.
- Rotate slowly.

Tip

Breathe out slowly so water does not go up your nose.

a.

b.

Layout Drill

Purpose

To practice the wrist action needed for all strokes.

Description

1. Float on your back with your toes pointed, feet together, and abdominals up. You will be traveling head first.
2. Keep your arms straight with your hands down at your sides and scull the water under the hips.
3. Use a quick wrist action.

Focus Points

- Keep your arms straight and focus on working the wrists.
- Keep your abdominals up.
- Keep your feet pointed and at the surface.
- Use quick hand action.

Variation

For an advanced version, try going feet first. Use just the wrists and try not to bend the elbows.

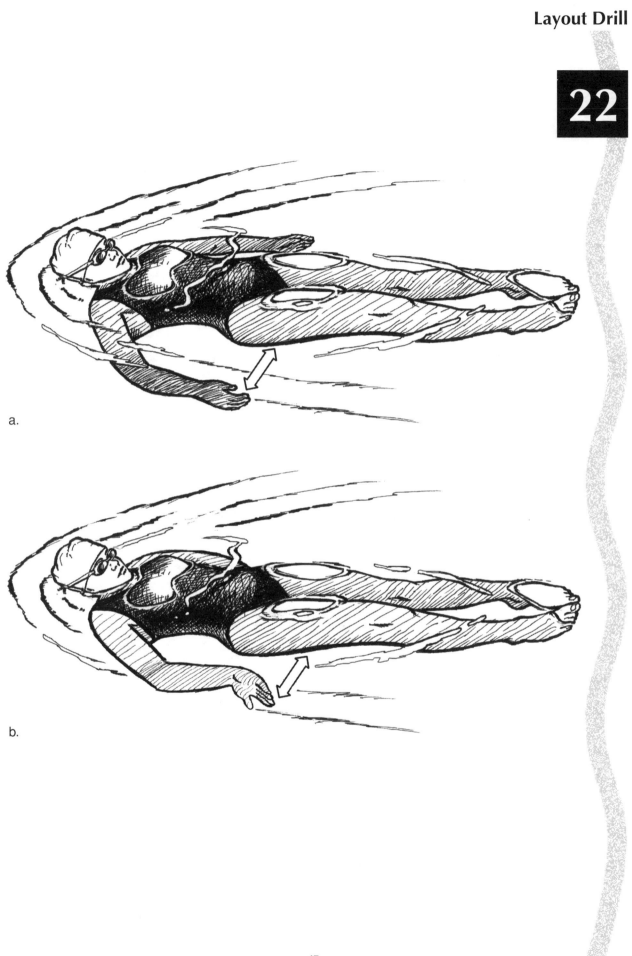

a.

b.

Seated Drill

Purpose

To practice the wrist action needed for all strokes.

Description

1. Begin by floating on your back, then tuck into a seated position.

2. Keep your knees and toes at the surface. Your head should be up as well.

3. Scull the water inward so that it travels under your knees. You will travel backward.

4. Use a quick wrist action.

Focus Points

- Keep your arms extended and focus on working the wrists.

- Keep your knees up at the surface.

- Stay in a seated position.

Variation

For an advanced version, travel feet first. Use just the wrists and try not to bend the elbows. In the forward direction, scoop backward under your hips.

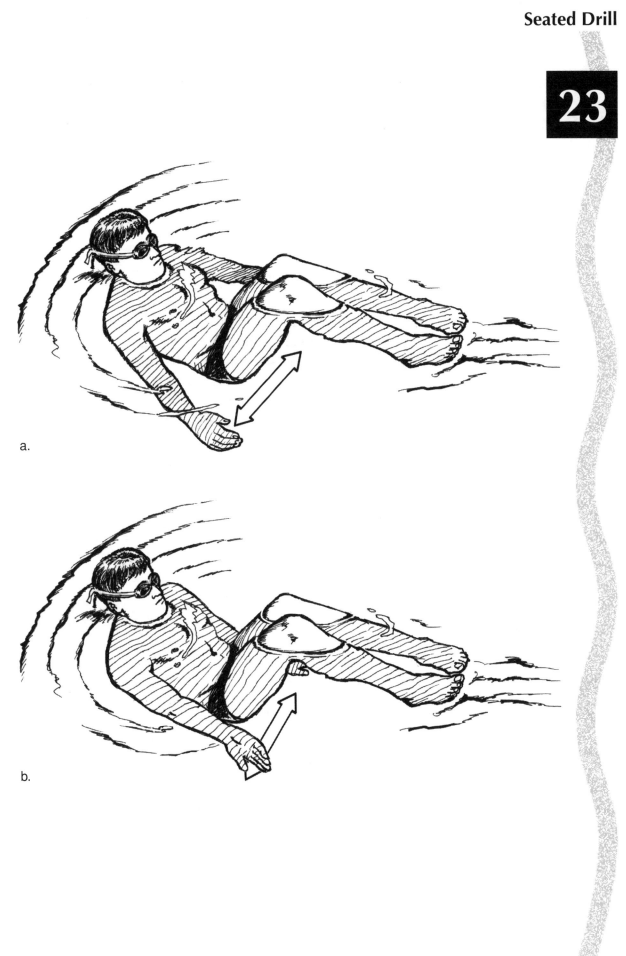

a.

b.

Elementary Backstroke Pull

Purpose

To practice the backstroke pulling action.

Description

1. Begin by floating flat on your back, traveling head first.
2. Keeping your hands under the water at all times, place your arms over your head, palms facing out.
3. Using both arms at the same time, pull downward past the shoulders, keeping the arms fairly straight.
4. Then begin to bend your elbows and turn your palms down toward your knees.
5. Keeping your hands close to the surface, continue to pull the water down toward your knees, and finish the pull with your thumbs against your thighs.
6. Then return your hands to the starting position by drawing them up alongside your body and stretching your arms overhead. Remember to keep your arms underwater.

Focus Points

- Pull evenly and slowly. Feel the pressure on the palms and forearms.
- Stay flat on your back with your abdominals up.

Tip

Use a pull buoy between your legs if it helps.

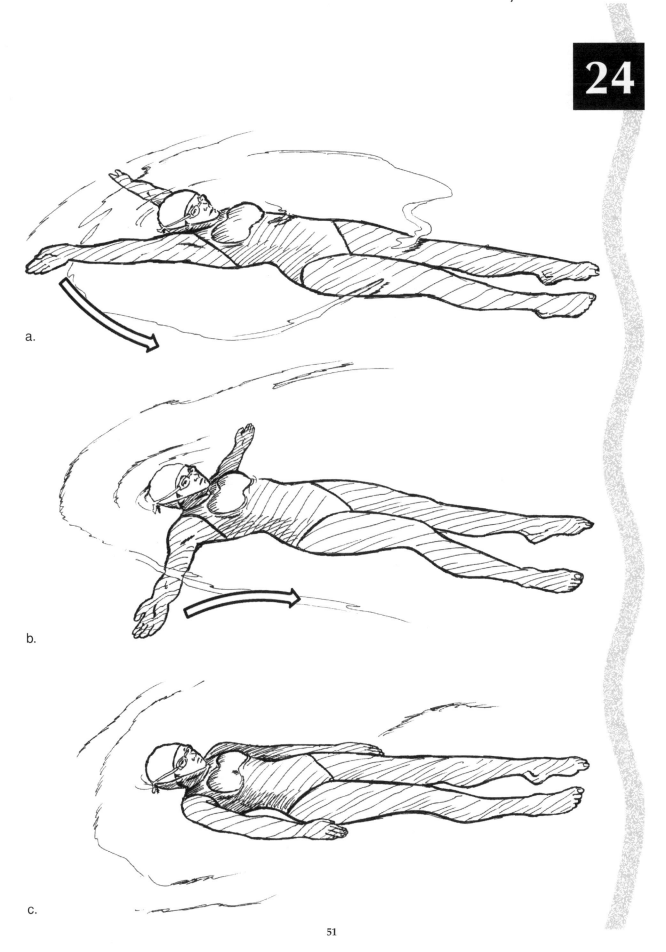

a.

b.

c.

25

Sea Otter

Purpose

To practice the feel of the finish of the strokes.

Description

1. Begin floating on your front side. You will travel head first. Keep your head up.

2. Place your arms down at your sides, keeping your elbows close to your ribs.

3. Bend your elbows so your hands are under your waist. Using your hands and forearms, scull the water backward, beginning at the waist.

4. There should be a small circular motion with the sculling. Move your hands very quickly.

Focus Points

- Keep your elbows in.
- Keep your head up as high as possible so that your eyes remain above the surface.
- Keep your hands under your waist.

Tips

- Using a pull buoy between your legs may help.
- Try sculling both forward and backward.

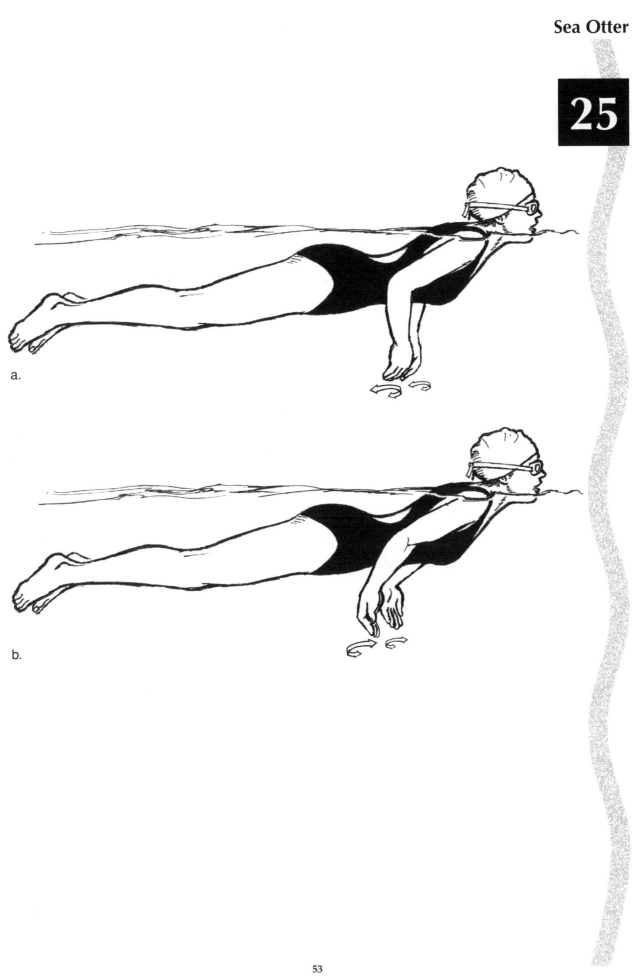

a.

b.

Dog Paddle

Purpose

To practice the feeling of the lift needed from the middle of the strokes.

Description

1. Begin floating on your front side, traveling head first. Keep your head up.
2. Your hands should be deep in the water, and your elbows should stay under your shoulders.
3. Bend your elbows and put your hands under your chin.
4. Alternating arms, scull down and back until your arms are straight and your hands are below your chest. Then bend your elbow and bring your hand up toward your body, then forward under your chin. Keep your hands above your waist and move them very quickly.

Focus Points

- Keep your elbows in a steady position under the shoulders.
- Keep your head up so that your eyes remain above the surface.
- Keep your hands above your waist.

Tip

Using a pull buoy between your legs may help.

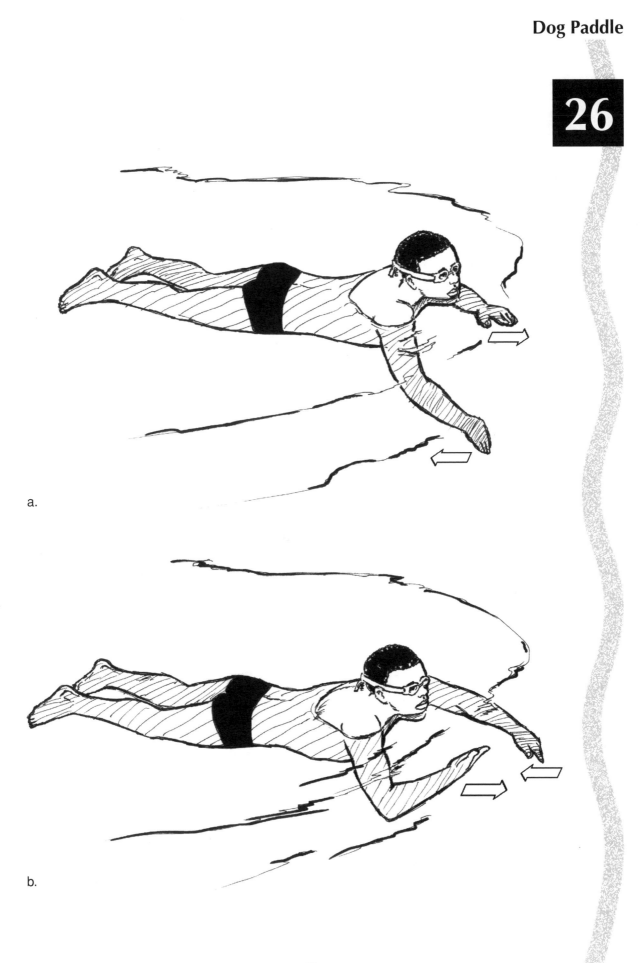

a.

b.

27

Front Scull

Purpose

To practice feeling the "catch" of the water at the beginning of the pulling action for the strokes.

Description

1. Begin floating on your front side traveling head first. Keep your head up.
2. Extend your arms in front of you. Sweep them out and then press them in using a wide motion.
3. Move your arms very quickly.
4. Bend your elbows slightly.

Focus Points

- Keep your arms extended and flex your elbows when pressing in.
- Keep your head up so that your eyes remain above the surface.
- Move your arms quickly.

Tips

- Using a pull buoy between your legs may help.
- For an advanced variation, try going backward (feet first).

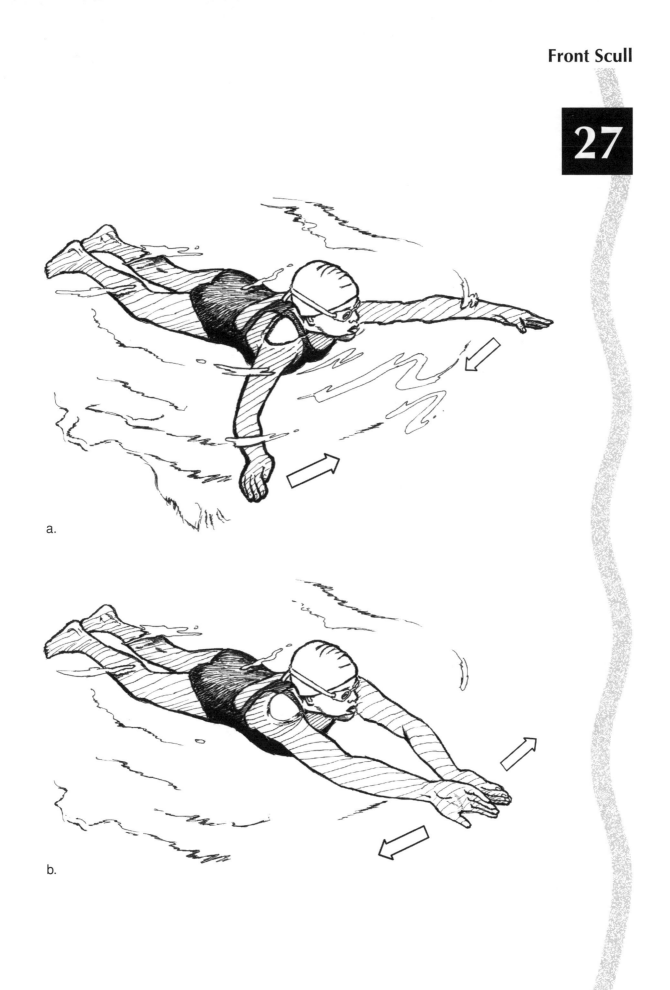

a.

b.

28

Scull and Kick

Purpose

To practice combining sculling and kicking.

Description

Repeat Drill 27 (Front Scull), but add a flutter kick.

Focus Points

- Keep your arms extended in front of you, sweeping out and pressing in.
- Keep your head up so that your eyes remain above the surface.
- Move your arms quickly.

Variation

For an advanced variation, do this backward or staying in place.

a.

b.

29

Lateral Scull

Purpose

To practice the pulling action of the freestyle and backstroke.

Description

1. Position your body on its side.
2. The top arm will not be used and should stay down at your side. Stretch your bottom arm out ahead of you.
3. Begin sculling, using a variety of actions—sideways, downward, and so on. Keep the hand action fast.
4. Keep your hand above the level of your shoulder.

Focus Points

- Move your hand quickly.
- Keep your body steady.

Tips

- Using a pull buoy between your legs may help.
- Try to combine the action of this drill with kicking.

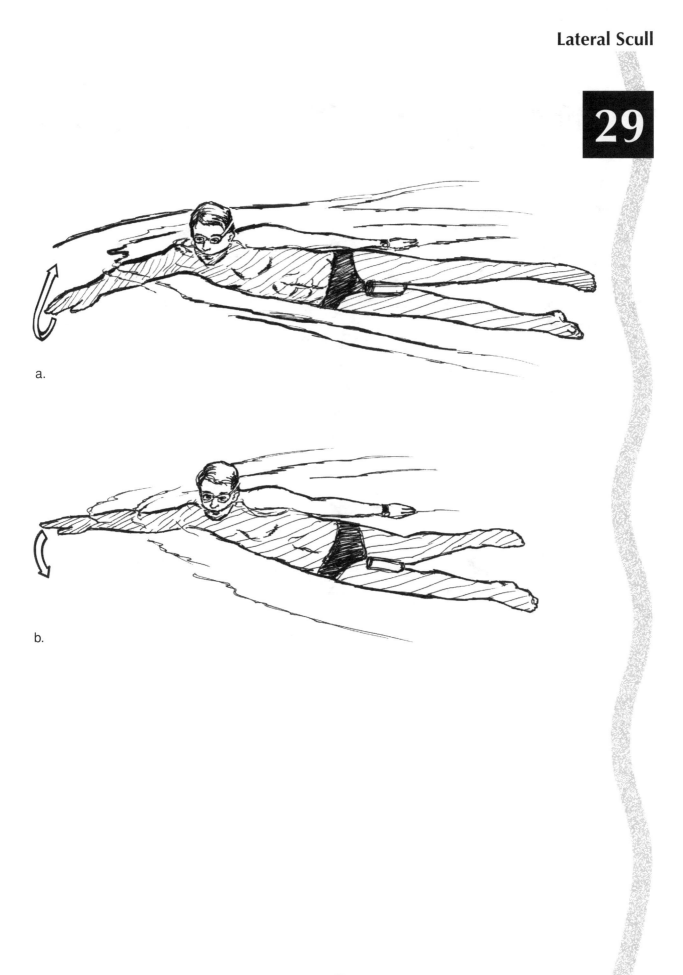

a.

b.

Brad Bridgewater in the 1997 Nissan Invitational, © Dan Helms

CHAPTER THREE

Backstroke

Backstroke is the only competitive stroke performed on the back. To execute it well requires not only sound technical skills, but also a high degree of comfort while swimming on one's back. In addition, safety must be assured to prevent injury.

The best backstrokers

- maintain excellent body position with the hips and torso up high;
- have a smooth, relaxed stroke recovery with the arms entering directly in line with the shoulders;
- have excellent head control, keeping the head steady;
- have good hip rotation, torso rolling, and shoulder lift;
- have flawless kicking, and
- pull through the water efficiently and with great power.

The drills presented in this chapter will help swimmers improve all of these fundamental aspects in their backstrokes.

Backstroke Recovery Deck Drill

Purpose

To isolate and emphasize the arm action of the backstroke recovery.

Description

1. Stand next to a wall that is taller than you are when your arms are stretched above your head.

2. Position your body with your side to the wall, so that your shoulder is 1 or 2 inches from the wall.

3. You will be using just the arm next to the wall. Keep that arm close to the wall at all times during this drill.

4. Start with your arm straight and palm against your thigh. Keeping your arm straight, lift it up as if you were to shake hands with an imaginary person in front of you.

5. Rotate your arm inward at the shoulder, keeping the elbow straight and turning your palm down. By the time your hand is as high as your head, your palm should be facing down on top of an imaginary person's head.

6. Continue to rotate your palm as you lift your arm until the arm is directly overhead. When your arm is straight up, the palm should be facing the wall. Repeat this movement several times. Begin slowly and gradually build up speed.

Focus Points

- "Paint" a large arc with your fingers as you do this drill.
- Perform this slowly with great control.
- Stay close to the wall.

Tip

Practice at home in front of a mirror.

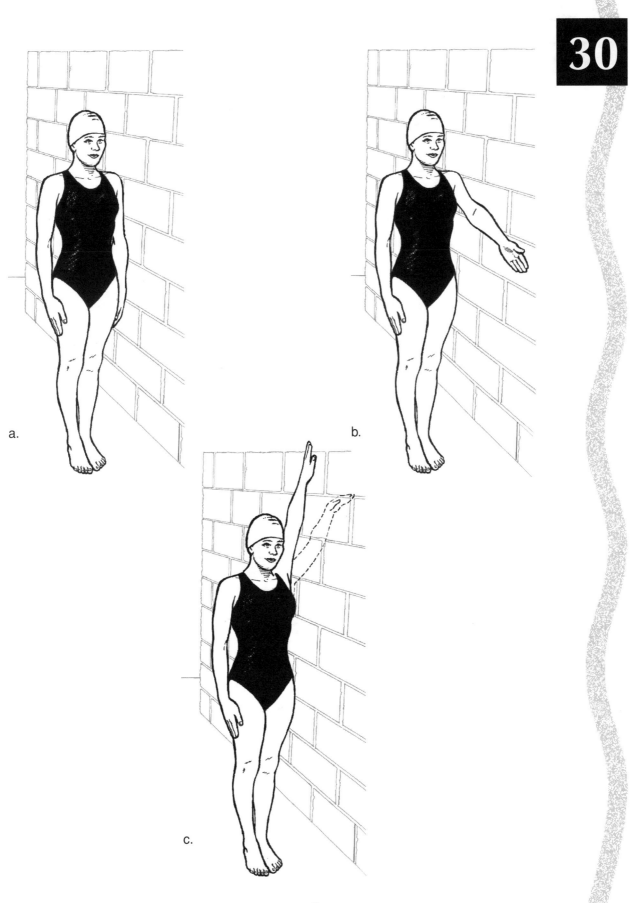

30

a.

b.

c.

31

One-Arm Streamline Kick

Purpose

To practice the streamline phase of the backstroke, with control of the body and hand positions. This is the first key drill in the backstroke series.

Description

1. Put fins on. Begin by pushing off the wall on your back with just one arm above your head in a streamline position.
2. Keep your other arm down at your side. Your up hand should be positioned with the palm facing outward with the thumb at the surface and the pinky toward the bottom. Your elbow should be straight.
3. Use a flutter kick and move along the surface.
4. Keep your head steady and the shoulder of your down arm above the surface.

Focus Points

- The head should remain stationary. Keep the ears level, just below the surface.
- Keep the shoulder of your down arm up high enough so that you can barely see the top of it from the bottom edge of your peripheral vision.
- Keep your shoulders steady.
- Control the position of your hand above your head so the palm faces out.

Tips

- For the hand position, think of the thumb as a periscope and make sure you keep the periscope up.
- For an advanced version, stay as close to the wall as possible, with your arm traveling against the wall. You could also use a lane rope as a guide, and brush the base of your palm along the lane rope. But the wall is best for this one.

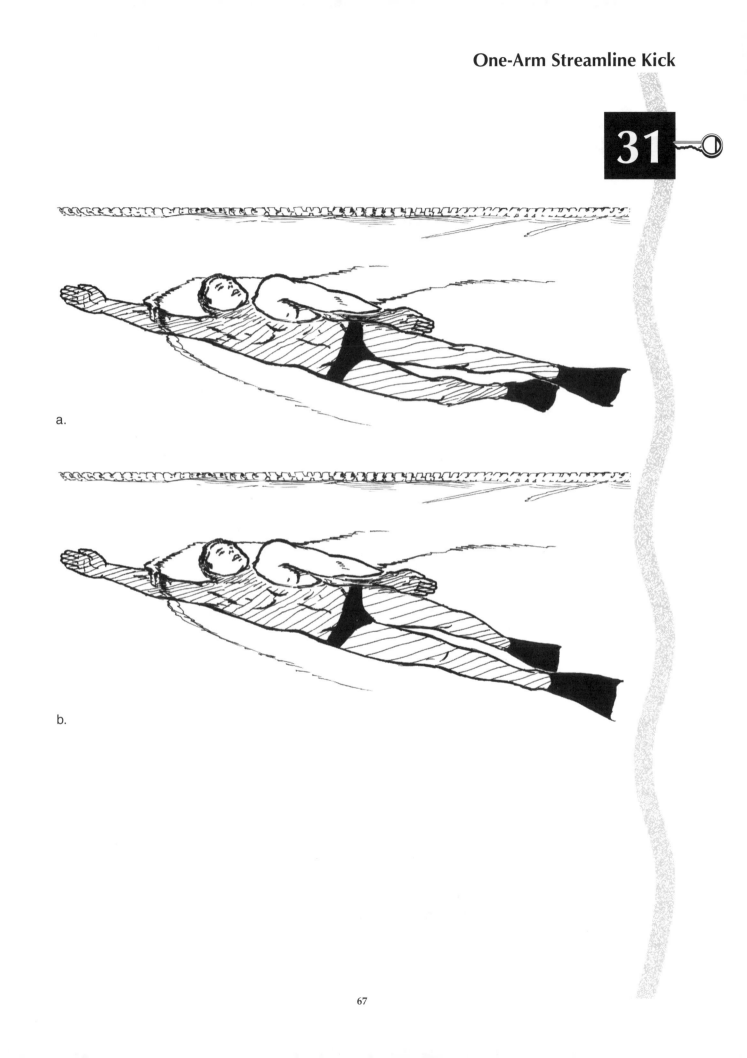

a.

b.

32

Shoulder Rotation

Purpose

To isolate and emphasize the shoulder rotation action of the backstroke.

Description

1. Because this drill requires strong kicking, put your fins on.

2. Begin by floating on your back and flutter kicking with your arms down at your sides. Keeping the head position steady, slowly begin to roll one shoulder up and out of the water as high as you can.

3. Allow your whole body to roll to the side, from the neck down. You should be able to see the top of your shoulder from the edge of your peripheral vision.

4. Once you reach the highest point possible, slowly begin to roll the opposite shoulder up.

5. Continue repeating the motion on both sides. Once you pass the backstroke flags at the other end of the pool, put one arm up above your head so that you can finish safely at the wall. (The flags on either end of the pool, called "backstroke flags" are there to help you turn or finish properly.)

Focus Points

- Keep your head steady.
- Roll slowly. It is not important how fast you do this drill, only how well you do it!
- Keep the kicking quick and constant.
- Roll your body from side to side.

Variation

For an advanced version, get into deep water and position your body vertically. From the deck, have someone place his or her hands on both sides of your head and hold you just above the surface. Then work on rolling your shoulders back and forth. This creates a "washing machine" action.

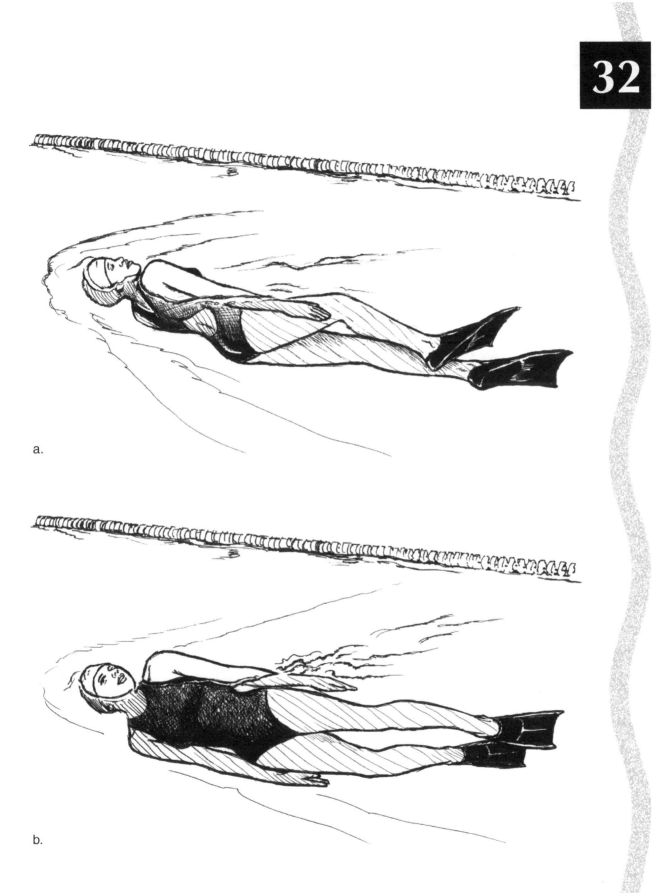

a.

b.

Guided One-Arm Backstroke

Purpose

To emphasize the backstroke pulling action in combination with the recovery and rolling actions.

Description

1. Put your fins on. Start by flutter kicking in a one-arm streamline backstroke position with the up arm right next to the lane rope. Hold this position for a count of three.

2. You will be using only the arm that is next to the lane rope; the other arm will stay down at your side.

3. Grab the lane rope. Gently pull your body along the rope, completing the pull down at your thigh.

4. As you complete the pull, you should "pop" up the shoulder of the pulling arm well above the surface. Hold this position for a count of three while you continue kicking.

5. Then slowly recover the pulling arm by lifting it through the air, with your hand traveling in a large arc until it enters the water overhead. Your hand should enter the water next to the lane rope, with the "periscope" thumb up.

6. As your hand enters the water, you should "pop" up the opposite shoulder. This completes one cycle.

7. Continue to repeat this cycle. Be sure to keep your arm above your head when you pass the flags so that you finish safely at the wall.

8. You should follow this pattern: *1, 2, 3, pull, pop, 4, 5, 6, recover, pop.*

Focus Points

- You should have one shoulder "popped" out at all times.
- Stay very close to the lane rope.
- Perform the drill slowly.
- Keep the kicking quick and strong.

Tip

Recite the pattern to yourself as you do the drill: *1, 2, 3, pull, pop, 4, 5, 6, recover, pop.*

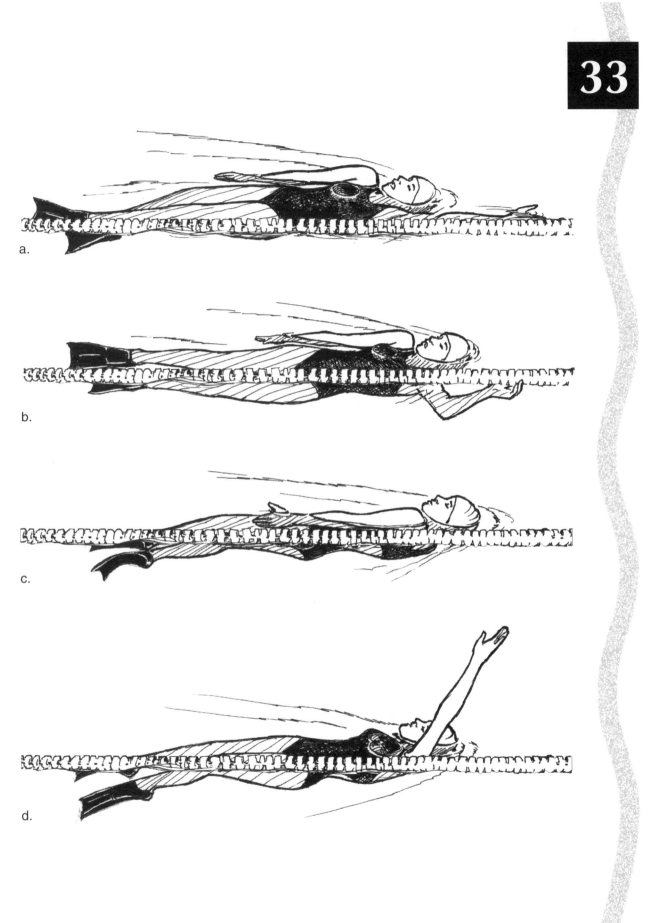

a.

b.

c.

d.

Controlled One-Arm Backstroke

Purpose

To develop the complete backstroke action with control. This is the second key drill in the backstroke series.

Description

This drill is performed exactly like the previous drill, except that the lane rope is not used for pulling. The pulling action will be along an imaginary lane rope that is about 1 foot deep.

1. Put your fins on. Start by kicking in a one-arm streamline position right next to the real lane rope with the up arm next to the rope. Hold this position for a count of three.

2. You will be using only the arm that is next to the lane rope; the other arm will stay down at your side.

3. Pull *under* the lane rope along an imaginary lane rope and complete the pull down at your thigh.

4. As you complete the pull, you should pop up the shoulder of the pulling arm well above the surface. Hold this position for a count of three while you continue kicking.

5. Then slowly recover the pulling arm. Your hand should enter the water next to the lane rope, with the "periscope" thumb up.

6. As your hand enters the water, you should pop up the opposite shoulder. This completes one cycle.

7. Continue to repeat this cycle. Be sure to keep your arm above your head when you pass the flags so that you finish safely at the wall.

8. Remember the pattern: *1, 2, 3, pull, pop, 4, 5, 6, recover, pop.*

Focus Points

- You should have one shoulder out at all times.
- Stay within 2 inches of the lane rope.
- Keep the kicking quick and strong.

Tip

Recite the cycle to yourself as you do the drill: *1, 2, 3, pull, pop, 4, 5, 6, recover, pop.*

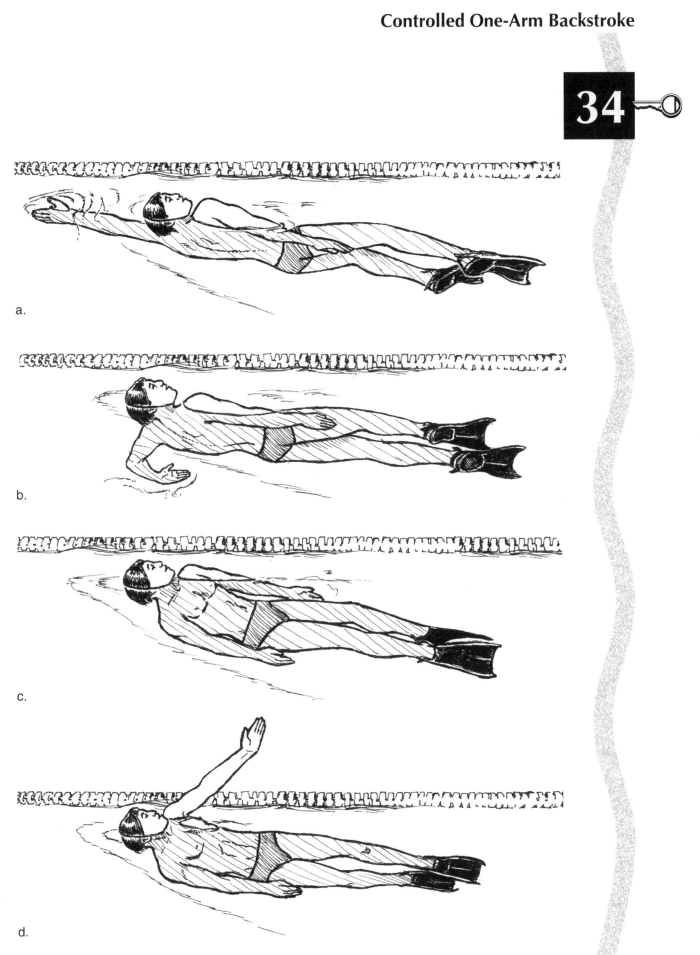

a.

b.

c.

d.

35

Double-Arm Backstroke

Purpose

To encourage the development of bent-elbow backstroke pulling.

Description

1. Put your fins on. Begin by flutter kicking on your back with both arms down at your sides. Hold this position for a count of three.

2. Then recover both arms at the same time. Once the hands enter the water, hold this position, with your arms stretched overhead and your hands barely underwater, for a count of three.

3. Pull both arms at the same time and finish at your side. This completes one cycle.

4. Continue to repeat this cycle. Be sure to keep your arms above your head when you pass the flags so that you finish safely at the wall.

Focus Points

- Keep your body position steady. Avoid any bouncing.
- Perform the drill slowly.
- Keep the kicking quick and strong.

Tips

- Think of pulling on imaginary lane ropes that are very close to either side of you.
- For an advanced version, perform this drill with a pull buoy between your legs and keep your body position very steady.

a.

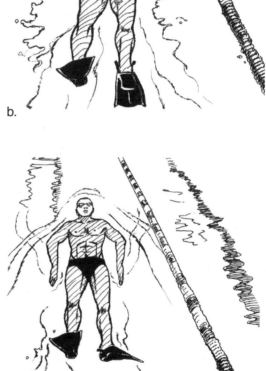

b.

c.

d.

36

Controlled Two-Arm Backstroke

Purpose

To develop the complete backstroke action with control and coordination of both arms. This is the third key drill in the backstroke series.

Description

This drill is the same as Drill 34 (Controlled One-Arm Backstroke), except that in this drill you will use both arms.

1. Put your fins on. Start by kicking in a one-arm streamline position with the right arm up and the left arm down at your side.

2. Hold this position for a count of three. Then switch arms at the same time by pulling with the right arm and recovering with the left arm until you reach the one-arm streamline position with the left arm up and right arm down.

3. Hold this streamline position for a count of three. Then repeat the switch. This completes one stroke cycle.

4. Continue to repeat this cycle. Be sure to keep your arm above your head when you pass the flags so that you finish safely at the wall.

Focus Points

- Keep one shoulder up at all times.
- Perform the drill slowly and smoothly.
- Keep the kicking quick and strong.

Tip

Switch both arms at the same time. Imagine a teeter-totter—let your shoulders rock back and forth with that motion. Let the shoulders lead the way. Rotate the shoulders first, then the arms.

36

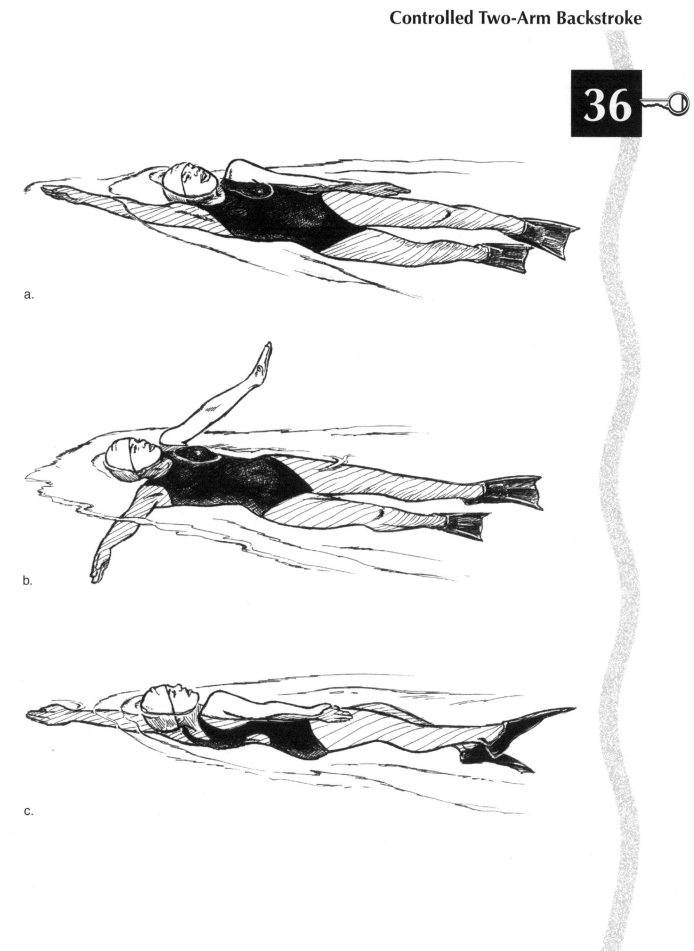

a.

b.

c.

37

Continuous One-Arm Backstroke

Purpose

To emphasize stroke control and body roll with the focus on just one arm. This is the fourth key drill in the backstroke series.

Description

This drill is performed exactly like Drill 34 (Controlled One-Arm Backstroke), except that there is no pausing between strokes.

1. Put your fins on. Start in a one-arm streamline position. You will use the arm above your head, and the other arm will stay down at your side.
2. Using a continuous action, pull and recover one arm.
3. Concentrate on excellent shoulder and body roll, and a steady head position.
4. Be sure to keep one arm above your head when you pass the flags so that you finish safely at the wall.

Focus Points

- Keep one shoulder out at all times.
- Perform the stroke smoothly. Do not pause at any point in the stroke.
- Keep the kicking quick and strong.

Tip

Watch your shoulders and rotate each one out as high as possible. Remember to imagine that teeter-totter movement.

37

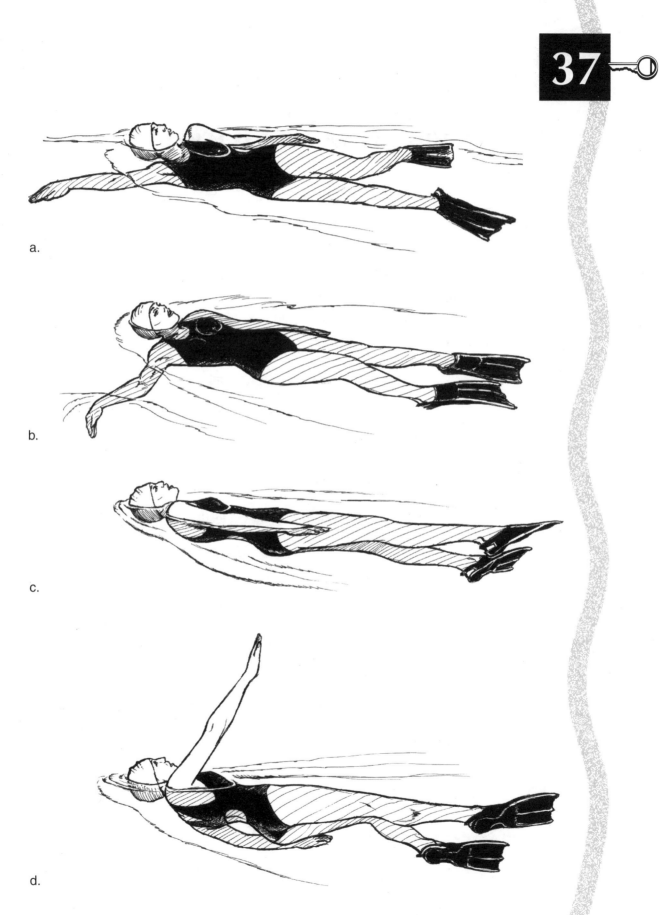

a.

b.

c.

d.

38

Continuous Two-Arm Backstroke

Purpose

To emphasize stroke control and body roll with the coordination of using both arms. This is the fifth and final key drill in the backstroke series.

Description

This drill is performed exactly like Drill 37 (Continuous One-Arm Backstroke), except that you will use both arms at the same time.

1. Put your fins on. Start by kicking in a one-arm streamline position.

2. Using a smooth continuous action, switch both arms at the same time.

3. Let the shoulders lead the arm action. Lift the shoulders high on the recovery. Do not pause at any point in the stroke.

4. Continue to repeat the cycle. Be sure to place one arm into the water above your head when you pass the flags so that you finish safely at the wall.

Focus Points

- Keep one shoulder out at all times.
- Perform the stroke smoothly. Do not pause at any point in the stroke.
- Keep the kicking quick and strong.

Tip

Watch your shoulders and rotate each one out as high as possible. Remember to imagine that teeter-totter movement.

38

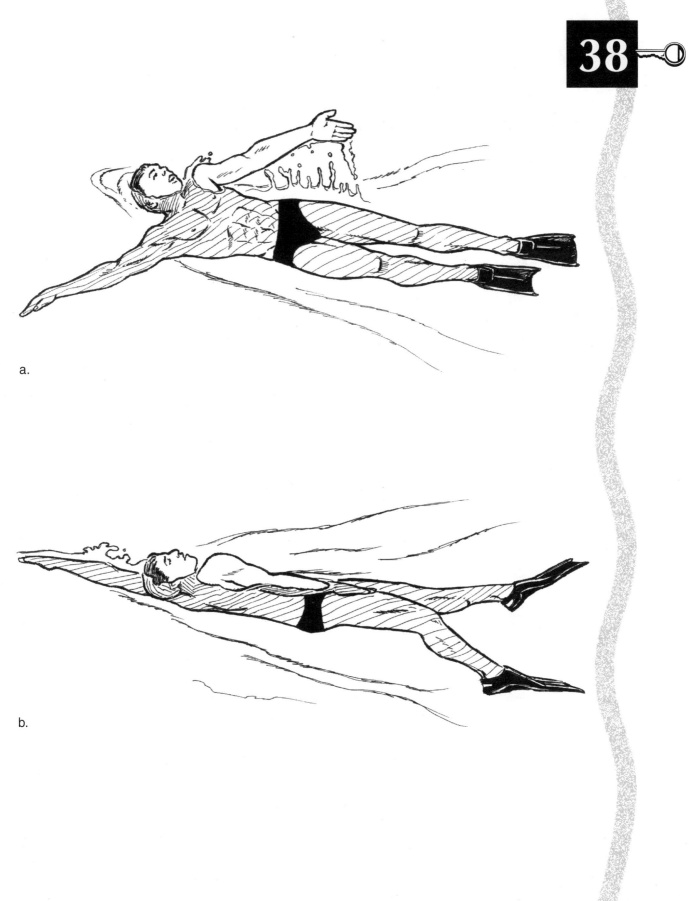

a.

b.

Backstroke Final Adjustment

Purpose

To practice the backstroke, focusing particularly on correct position of the hands as they enter the water.

Description

1. Now that you have excellent shoulder and body roll in the backstroke, you will be able to swim the stroke with what *feels* like a wider stroke.

2. For most swimmers, the hands should feel like they are entering the water at the 10 o'clock and 2 o'clock positions. This will feel deceptively easy, and if the stroke is correct, it should.

3. Swim a smooth, controlled backstroke, concentrating on feeling your hands enter the water at the 10 and 2 positions. You may also notice that the stroke will move a little quicker. This is OK. Be sure you keep the good shoulder roll, steady body position, and strong kicking.

4. Have your coach or training partner stand on the deck at the end of your lane to see if your hands enter the water right above your shoulders. There should be no over-reaching or underreaching. The most common problem is overreaching (when the hands enter past the line of the respective shoulder; for example, if the hand enters directly over the head.) Make adjustments as necessary.

Focus Points

- Make sure your hands feel like they enter the water at 10 o'clock and 2 o'clock.
- Don't forget to maintain all of the correct mechanics of the backstroke—steady body position, quick and strong kicking, and a good shoulder roll.

Tip

Swimming next to the lane rope is another way to check your arm entry position. Your hand should enter the water right next to the lane rope. Also, while swimming next to the lane rope, perform a few strokes with your eyes closed to help you really feel the stroke.

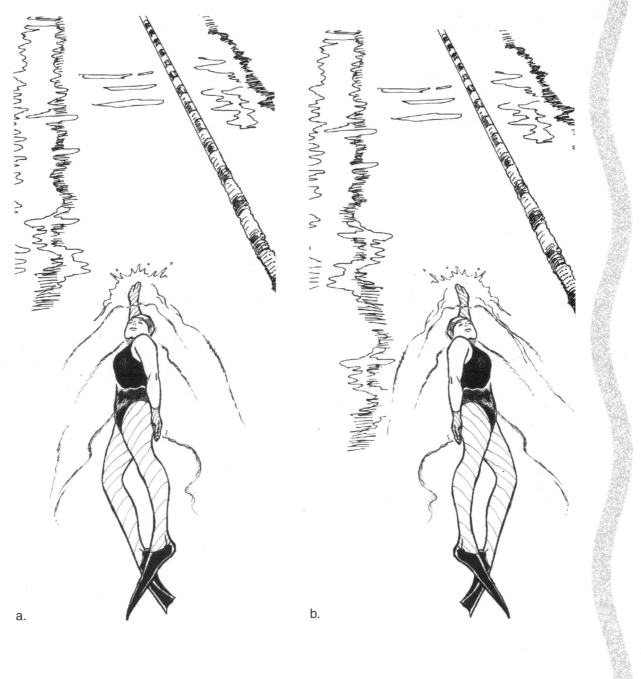

a.

b.

Matt Biondi in a 1992 meet sponsored by Alamo Car Rental, © Dan Helms

CHAPTER FOUR

Freestyle

Freestyle is the fastest of the competitive strokes. However, in competition swimmers often try to speed up their time by moving their arms faster through the air, trying so hard that their strokes actually deteriorate and slow them down. Swimmers must maintain a balance of good technique, and strong pulling and kicking in order to move faster.

The best freestylers

- maintain excellent head and body position with their bodies high out of the water;
- have a smooth, relaxed stroke recovery with the elbows high and hands traveling close to the body;
- have excellent head control and breathe comfortably;
- have good hip rotation, torso rolling, and shoulder lift;
- have flawless kicking; and
- pull through the water efficiently and with great power.

The drills in this chapter will help swimmers apply these characteristics of the best freestylers to their own strokes.

40

Freestyle Breathe and Kick

Purpose

To isolate the breathing action of the freestyle and practice control of the body position and head position. This is the first key drill in the freestyle series. Review Drill 7 (Lateral Kick).

Description

1. Put your fins on. Hold a half-board at the bottom, with your fingers on top of the board and your thumb wrapped underneath. Keep the other arm down at your side.

2. Begin kicking while looking forward with your eyes right at the surface. Hold this position for a count of three. Be sure to blow a steady stream of bubbles.

3. Roll your body to the same side of the arm that is up.

4. Rotate at the shoulder of the arm that is holding the board. When you complete your roll, the other shoulder should be up as high as possible (perpendicular to the surface of the water) and your body will be on its side.

5. Rest your head comfortably on the surface of the water so that your ear is just under the water and the edge of your eye is at the surface. The corner of your mouth will be just under the surface. Inhale.

6. After inhaling, return to the forward position and repeat the cycle. Be sure to keep your eyes at the surface.

Focus Points

- Keep the eyes up and at the surface. Resist the temptation to look down—a very common error that will drive your body down in the water and increase drag tremendously, thereby slowing you down and wasting your energy.

- Roll the body, not the neck. Lift that shoulder up high.

- Control your head position.

- Look across the surface of the pool when you breathe in.

Tip

Practice this on both sides so that you will learn to be comfortable with alternate breathing (see Drill 41, Underwater Recovery With Alternate Breathing).

a.

b.

41

Underwater Recovery With Alternate Breathing

Purpose

To introduce the rhythm of alternate breathing and the proper timing of the breathing cycle. This is also a good drill for practicing freestyle pulling.

Description

1. Before starting this drill, think of how a teeter-totter works. In this drill, your arms will be moving in opposite directions at the same time, much like a teeter-totter. One arm will be forward and the other arm will be back.

2. Put your fins on. Begin kicking and stretch one arm out in front of you and place the other arm down at your side with your palm against your leg. Keep your head forward and your eyes up near the surface of the water.

3. Keeping your arms completely under the water, begin to switch your arm positions back and forth. Each time you switch, stretch your arm out as fully as possible. Remember to keep the shoulder of your down arm above the water.

4. When you reach the stretched position, count *one*. Switch again and count *two*. As you switch the third time, roll to your side to breathe. When you reach *three* you should be completely on your side with your head positioned as in the previous drill. Return your head to the forward position as you begin to switch, and then count *one* again. Continue to repeat the cycle.

Focus Points

- Keep your head high.
- Reach a complete stretch each time.
- Get your shoulder up on each stretch.
- Perform the drill smoothly and with control.

Tip

Play a waltz in your head and keep time to the three-beat music. Always breathe on the third beat!

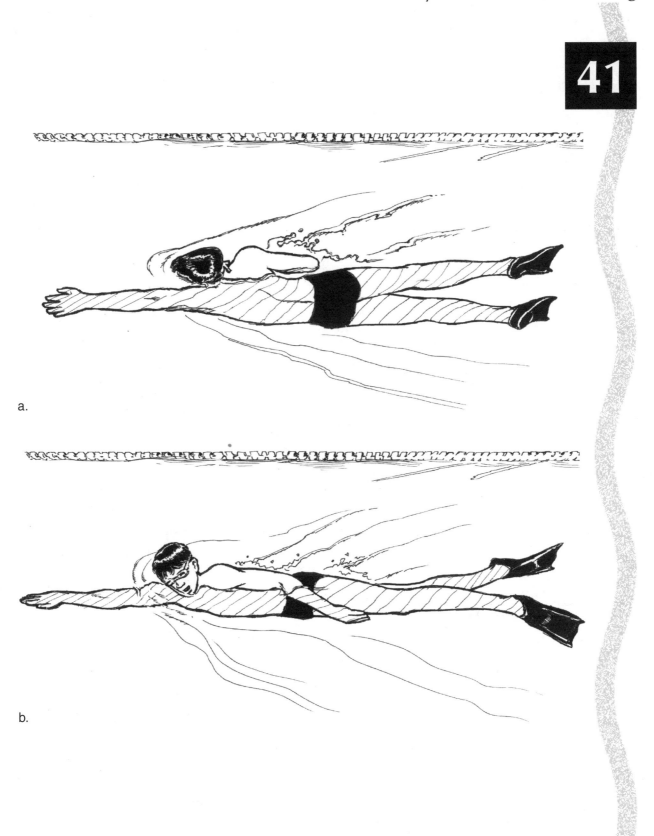

a.

b.

42

Zip-Up

Purpose

To emphasize the proper mechanics for the arm recovery. This drill is excellent for helping swimmers with chronic shoulder problems retrain their strokes.

Description

1. Put your fins on. Begin by practicing Drill 7 (Lateral Kick); hold a half-board across the top with one arm, kick on your side, control your head position, and keep your shoulder up high.

2. Place your hand down at your side so that the back of your hand is against your thigh. Then grab an imaginary zipper between your thumb and forefinger and pull the zipper up along your body until you reach your armpit.

3. Your thumbnail should stay against your body, pointing toward the middle of your body. Your palm should remain face up. As you pull up, your wrist should be relaxed and your elbow should come straight up.

4. Once you complete the lifting action, slowly return the arm in the same manner to the starting position. Continue to repeat this cycle. Be sure to practice on both sides.

Focus Points

- Keep the shoulder position high.
- Perform this drill slowly and with control.
- Lift the elbow straight up as you pull up.
- Remember to keep good head position and kicking.

Tip

Try doing this while facing a lane rope or high wall. Keep your hand next to your body. This will force you to recover properly.

a.

b.

43

Controlled One-Arm Freestyle

Purpose

To isolate the proper mechanics of the freestyle, one arm at a time. This is the second key drill in the freestyle series.

Description

1. Put your fins on. Hold a half-board with one hand. Place your other hand (which will be pulling) under the board with the knuckles against the board. Keep your head forward and your eyes just at or barely under the surface. Kick forward and hold this position for a count of three as you blow bubbles.

2. After counting to three, begin to pull your arm down and roll your body. As your hand passes under your shoulder, your head should begin turning to the side to breathe.

3. Complete the pull in the "open" position, the same position as in Drill 7 (Lateral Kick). As you finish the pull, the palm will be facing up. Hold this open position for an additional count of three.

4. Then begin the zip-up action to bring your elbow up. As your hand reaches your shoulder, begin to return your head to the forward position. (The hand should *not* pass in front of your face on the recovery.)

5. Pass the hand forward so that it slices into the water just in front of the half-board. Then slide the hand under the half-board to complete the cycle. Practice with each arm.

6. Repeat this cycle to yourself as you perform the drill: *1, 2, 3, pull, breathe, open, 4, 5, 6, elbow, head, hand.*

Focus Points

• Keep your head high.
• Keep the kicking steady.
• Concentrate on one step at a time.

Variation

For an advanced version, perform this drill next to a lane rope. Use the top of the rope as a guide for your hand when recovering your arm. Let the fingernails of your first and middle fingers gently glide across the top of the lane rope as if it were a piano.

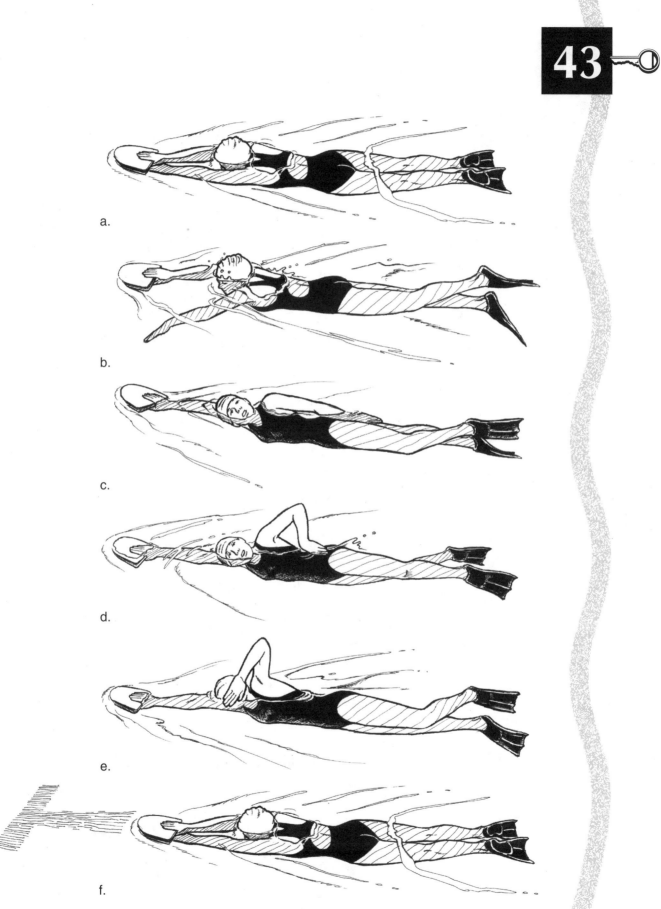

43

a.

b.

c.

d.

e.

f.

Controlled Two-Arm Freestyle

Purpose

To develop the coordinated two-arm freestyle action with control of the timing. This drill will also allow the swimmer to feel the complete extension of the freestyle stroke. This is the third key drill in the freestyle series.

Description

1. Put your fins on. Start by kicking in a one-arm streamline position with the left arm up and the right arm down at your side. The shoulder of your right arm will be above the water. Keep your head looking forward, and remember to blow bubbles. Hold this position for a count of three.

2. Then switch arms at the same time by pulling with the left arm and recovering with the right arm until you reach a one-arm streamline position with the right arm up and the left arm down. Hold this position for a count of three.

3. Repeat the switch. This completes one stroke cycle. Continue to repeat this cycle.

4. To practice proper freestyle breathing, start off breathing to just one side for several laps, then on the other side for several laps. Eventually work up to breathing every third stroke. In other words, *1, 2, breathe, 1, 2, breathe.*

Focus Points

- Keep your head forward and your eyes up near the surface.
- You should have one shoulder up each time you hold the stretched position.
- Perform the drill slowly and smoothly.
- Keep the kicking quick and strong.

Variation

For an advanced version, perform this drill next to a lane rope. Use the top of the rope as a guide for one of your arms as you perform this drill. On the recovery, allow your fingernails to glide across imaginary piano keys on the rope.

44

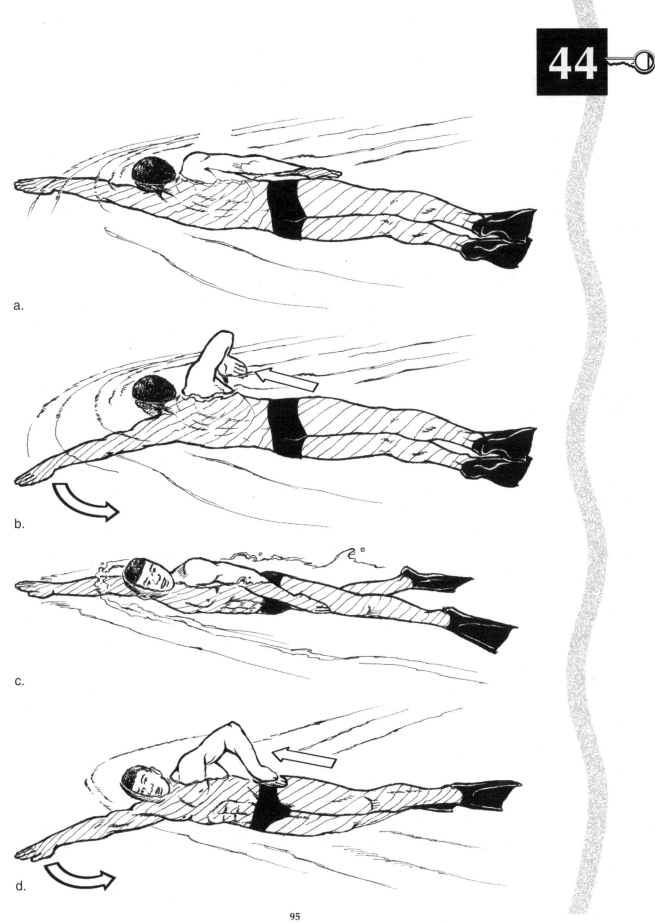

a.

b.

c.

d.

45

Continuous One-Arm Freestyle

Purpose

To isolate the proper mechanics of the freestyle, one arm at a time. In order to execute this drill properly, swimmers will need to have excellent kicking and stroke control. This is the fourth key drill in the freestyle series.

Description

The action of this drill is very similar to that of Drill 37 (Continuous One-Arm Backstroke). Remember to move your shoulders back and forth continuously in a teeter-totter action.

1. Put your fins on and start on your front in a one-arm streamline position. Use the arm in front and keep the other arm down at your side.

2. Using a continuous action, pull and recover the one arm you are working. Concentrate on excellent shoulder roll and steady head position.

3. Breathe on the same side that you are pulling. Roll the opposite shoulder so that it completely breaks the surface and reaches a nearly perpendicular angle to the surface.

4. Repeat the action for the other arm.

Focus Points

- Push each shoulder out nice and high.
- Keep the head and body positions steady.
- Perform the stroke slowly and smoothly. Do not pause at any point in the stroke.
- Get full extension on every stroke. Reach all the way forward, and pull all the way back.
- Keep the kicking quick and strong.

Tips

- Feel the shoulder and upper arm of your down arm come above the surface when you extend the pulling arm forward.
- For an advanced version, try this drill with no fins.

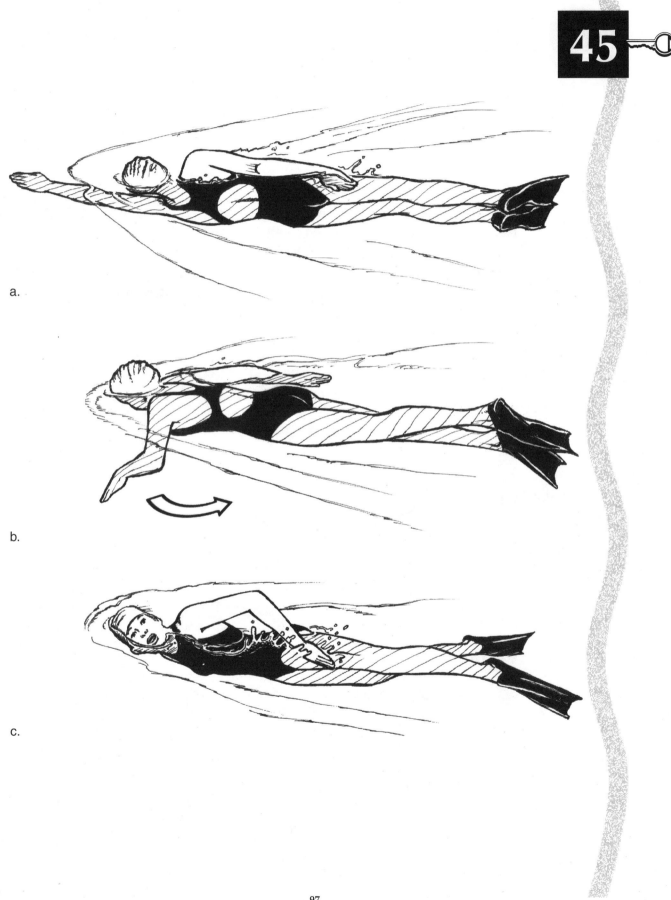

a.

b.

c.

46

Continuous Two-Arm Freestyle

Purpose

To emphasize stroke control and shoulder roll with the coordination of using both arms. This is the fifth and final key drill in the freestyle series.

Description

This drill is performed exactly like Drill 45 (Continuous One-Arm Freestyle) except that you will use both arms at the same time.

1. Put your fins on and start by kicking in a one-arm streamline position.

2. Using a smooth continuous action, switch both arms at the same time. Do not pause at any point in the stroke. However, be sure to reach full extension and to complete each pull.

3. Continue to repeat the cycle.

Focus Points

- Keep the head and body position steady.
- Feel the shoulder lift on each recovery.
- Perform the stroke slowly and smoothly. Do not pause at any point in the stroke.
- Get full extension on every stroke.
- Keep the kicking quick and strong.

Tips

- Try to watch your hands enter the water. Make sure they slice into the water and check whether you lose the air bubbles quickly. The fewer air bubbles, the better.
- Be sure to practice alternate breathing!

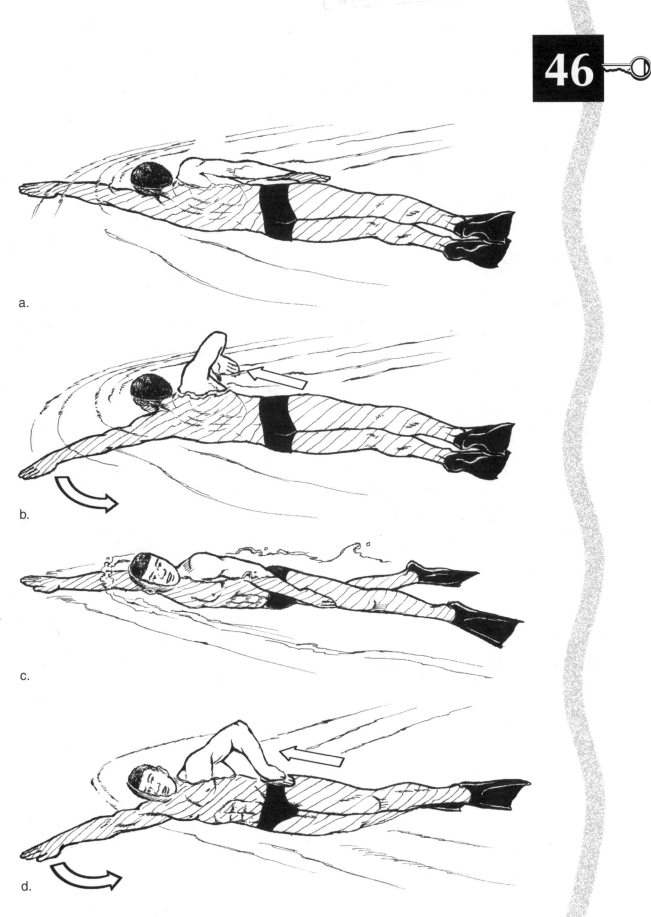

a.

b.

c.

d.

Mike Barrowman in a 1992 meet sponsored by Alamo Car Rental, © Dan Helms

CHAPTER FIVE

Breaststroke

The breaststroke offers perhaps the greatest variability in style among the strokes. There are almost as many styles of breaststroke as there are breaststroke coaches. However, there are some fundamentals common to almost all great breaststrokers.

The best breaststrokers

- reach a streamlined position, or glide, at least for an instant on every stroke, assuring full extension and maximum efficiency;
- pull using an outsweep, insweep, and recovery that accelerates from the beginning of the pull, and does not pause until the streamline is reached again;
- keep their hips high throughout the entire stroke;
- complete the kick with a strong squeeze and pointed toes; and
- maintain good head control, always keeping the chin tucked in.

The breaststroke drills on the following pages will teach swimmers these essential techniques for enhancing their strokes. Individual variations can then be developed once these fundamentals are mastered.

47

Vertical Breaststroke Pull

Purpose

To develop the correct mechanics for the breaststroke pull. This also enhances arm pull speed and helps swimmers who tend to overpull or who have a slow arm pull.

Description

1. Put your fins on and move out to deep water. Begin by flutter kicking in a vertical position. Keep your body straight and your head above the surface. Position your arms out in front of you so that your thumbs are touching and your palms are facing down and slightly out. Hold this position for a count of three.

2. Begin the pulling action by sweeping your hands outward just under the surface. You should reach a point where the fingers are still pointing forward (before they begin to point out to the sides) and your hands are apart about twice shoulder-width.

3. Rotate the hands inward, begin to bend the elbows in toward the chest, and sweep your hands in.

4. As your hands come together and your elbows come to your sides, shoot the hands forward at the surface. Extend your arms forward to the starting position.

5. As you sweep your arms out and then in, you should lift your body above the surface, at least to mid-chest height. Repeat the cycle.

Focus Points

- Keep your body straight.
- Pause only in the starting position.
- Accelerate and lift as you pull.
- Shoot your hands forward very quickly.

Tips

- Watch your hands as you perform this drill. You should always see them in front of your shoulders.
- Try to get your elbows against your sides, or squeeze your elbows together as you finish the pull.

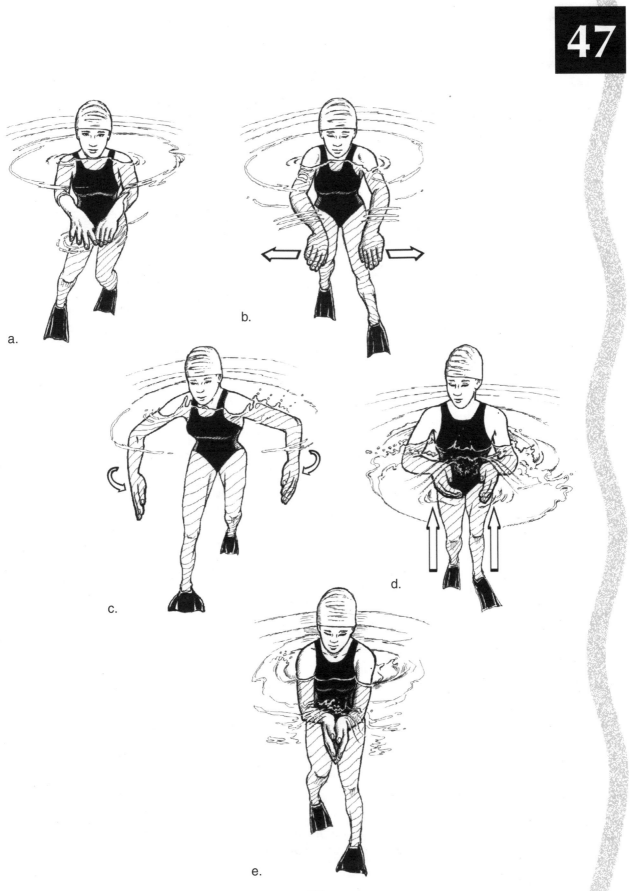

a.

b.

c.

d.

e.

48

Breaststroke Pull and Flutter Kick

Purpose

To isolate the proper mechanics of the breaststroke pull and to emphasize the necessary speed and lift for the stroke. This drill also focuses on control of the head position. This is the first key drill of the breaststroke series.

Description

1. Put your fins on and kick forward with your arms together in front of your body. Hold your arms together for a count of three. Then pull and recover quickly, using the breaststroke arm motion you practiced in Drill 47 (Vertical Breaststroke Pull).

2. Get plenty of lift while pulling. Return your head to the starting position (see variations of head position below). Continue to repeat the cycle.

3. There are three variations of the starting head position that you should practice: First, practice this drill with the chin starting at the surface, and keep the chin from going under the water. This variation emphasizes arm speed. In the second variation, the eyes should be just above the surface in the starting position. Keep your chin tucked in while pulling. Look downward at about a 45 degree angle, keeping the head angle steady. For the third variation, keep your eyes just below the surface in the starting position. Again, be sure to keep your chin tucked in while pulling. Look downward at 45 degrees, keeping the head angle steady.

Focus Points

- Be sure to breathe. Blow bubbles when your face is in the water. This allows you to breathe quickly when you pull.

- Keep your chin tucked in! Lift the body, not the chin.

- Really stretch and hold the extension for a count of three.

Tip

When your arms are out in front, you create a "window" that you can look through toward the bottom of the pool. Keep your chin tucked in so that you can always look through the top of the window. Your head angle remains steady.

48

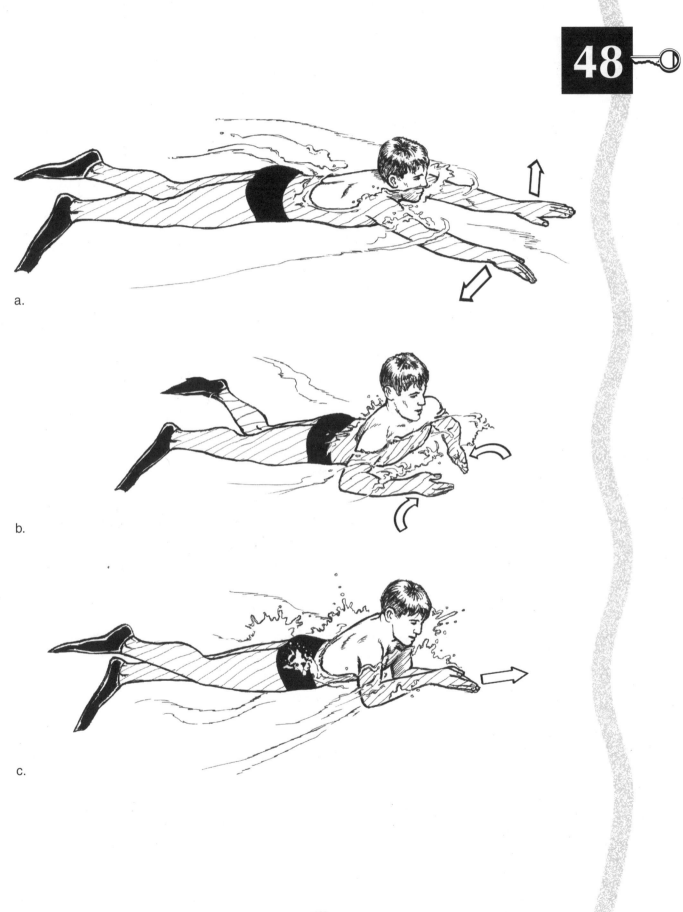

a.

b.

c.

Advanced Breaststroke Kick

Purpose

To isolate the breathing and kicking phases of the breast-stroke while allowing the swimmer to feel the streamline glide created after the power phase of the kick. This is the second key drill of the breaststroke series.

Description

1. Lock your thumbs together and extend your arms forward. Start by pushing off with your face in the water and your eyes just below the water. You should have your head at a 45 degree angle.

2. Stretch out into a glide position with the legs together, toes pointed, and hips up. Count to three. Be sure to blow bubbles the whole time your face is in the water.

3. Then lift your head up so that your chin is on the surface. Keep your hands forward. Breathe in and begin your kick, bringing the legs in. As you kick out and squeeze, lower your face into the water and begin to breathe out.

4. Complete the kick and lift your legs to the surface. Hold the glide for three, then repeat.

Focus Points

- Concentrate on this pattern: *breathe, kick, glide.*

- Feel how your body slices through the water when you kick and then glide.

- After you finish the glide, lift your head first.

- Keep your hands in a steady position, about 6 to 8 inches below the surface.

Tips

- Move across the pool with as few kicks as possible, and determine your average number of kicks.

- For an interesting variation, take only one breath for every two or three kicks. This really helps in developing the feel for the glide. Keep a low number of kicks per lap.

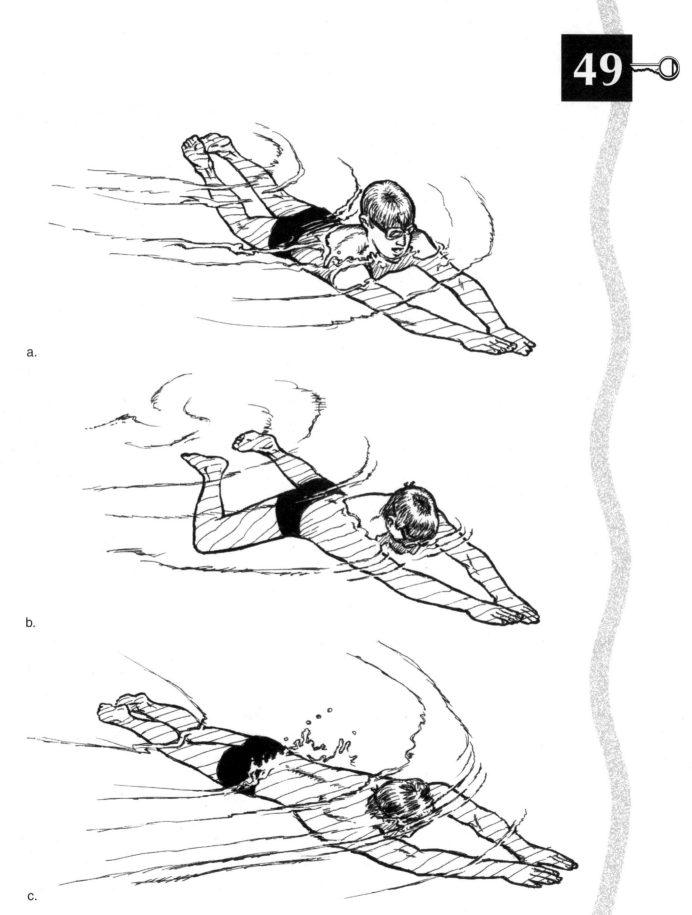

a.

b.

c.

Two Kicks to One Pull

Purpose

To develop the proper timing and extension of the breast-stroke. This is the third key drill in the breaststroke series.

Description

The kicking action is exactly the same as Drill 49 (Advanced Breaststroke Kick). Now the pulling action will be added to every other kick.

1. Follow this pattern: *pull, breathe, kick, glide* and then *breathe, kick, glide.* Hold each glide for a count of three.

2. Keep your head down, positioned at a 45 degree angle. On the glide, the top of your forehead should be at the surface.

3. You should end up with at least one less kick per lap than the number of kicks you used in Drill 49.

Focus Points

- Kick with an even rhythm.
- Keep your hands in a steady position when not pulling. Locking the thumbs helps.
- Keep the pull quick and get plenty of lift.
- Control your head position.

Tips

- Keep track of the number of kicks you take each lap. Determine your average. Try to decrease the number each time you practice this drill!
- For a variation, breathe only when you pull. This will help you keep a feel for the glide and extension.

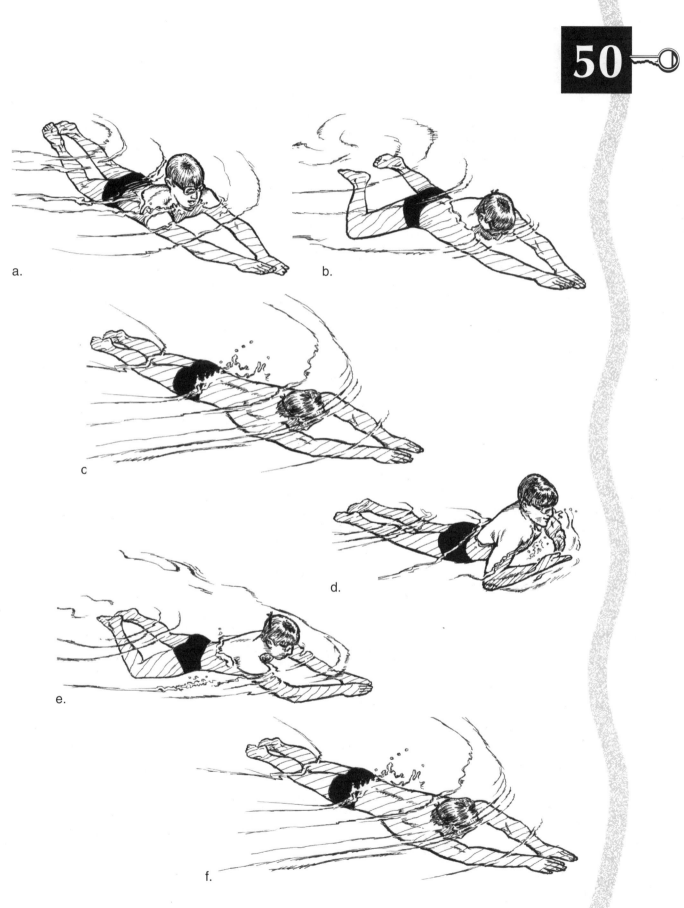

a.

b.

c.

d.

e.

f.

51

Eyes-Up Breaststroke

Purpose

To help swimmers develop the proper timing for the breast-stroke and a quick pulling action. This drill will help correct the common tendency of young swimmers to overpull and as a result, stop their pulling under the chest. This is the fourth key drill of the breaststroke series.

Description

1. In this drill, simply practice the breaststroke with one pull for each kick and glide. However, keep the eyes above the surface at all times. The chin should still be tucked in.
2. Follow this pattern: *pull, lift (breathe), kick, glide*.
3. Hold the glide for a count of three. You should be able to see your hands staying in front of you. If your eyes go under the water, you may be overpulling.

Focus Points

- Maintain an even rhythm.
- Hold the glide for a count of three.
- Keep your eyes up above the surface, but keep the chin in.
- Keep the pulling quick and get plenty of lift.

Tip

Keep track of the number of kicks you take each lap. Try to decrease the number each time you practice this drill!

a.

b.

52

Controlled Breaststroke

Purpose

To emphasize control along with the proper timing and extension for the breaststroke. This is the fifth key drill in the breaststroke series.

Description

1. In this drill, simply practice the breaststroke with one pull for each kick and glide. Follow this pattern: *pull, lift (breathe), kick, glide.*

2. Keep your head down, positioned at a 45 degree angle. On the glide, the top of your forehead should be at the surface.

3. Start off with a glide for a count of three. Count the number of strokes. You should end up with at least one less kick per lap than the average number of kicks from Drill 50 (Two Kicks to One Pull).

Focus Points

- Maintain an even rhythm.
- Hold the glide for a count of three.
- Keep the pull quick and get plenty of lift.
- Control the head position.

Tip

To get closer to the timing needed for the racing stroke, gradually reduce the length of time that you hold the glide position. The shorter the race, the quicker the glide; the longer the race, the longer the glide. Here are the glide times to shoot for in races:

- For the 200m, hold for a count of two to three.
- For the 100m, hold for a count of one to two.
- For the 50m, hold for a count up to one.

Coaches note: Once the swimmer masters the stroke with consistent head control, the head angle can be modified to allow for optimum body position on the glide. Keep in mind that there is a lot of individual variation possible in breaststroke.

52

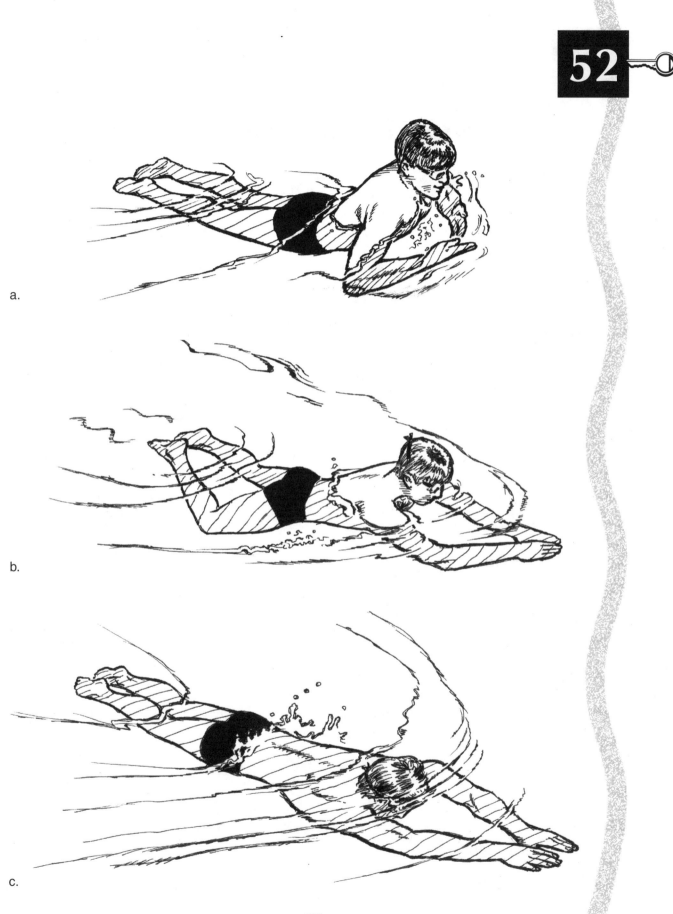

a.

b.

c.

Breaststroke Pull and Dolphin Kick

Purpose

To emphasize the hip action needed for the different dolphin breaststrokes by combining the breaststroke and butterfly. Not all swimmers will feel comfortable with this technique which uses more of a "dolphin" action with the hips. This is not a key drill, but for many swimmers, depending on their strengths and weaknesses, it may be extremely effective.

Description

1. Put your fins on. Start off on your front by dolphin kicking in a streamline position. Take a breaststroke pull, and breathe while you pull.

2. As you recover, push your hips up and then finish with the downward part of the dolphin kick. Be sure to stretch your arms out far in front of you. As you kick down, begin to pull again. Continue to repeat.

3. The rhythm of this drill will vary depending on your ease with the dolphin kick. For those who are very comfortable with this action, the rhythm can be quite quick.

Focus Points

- Stretch forward with your arms.
- Get your hips and legs up on every kick.
- Keep the pulling action quick.
- Try to stay up fairly high and resist going too deep under the surface.

Tip

To get a better sense of the proper rhythm, try breathing every other pull or every third pull.

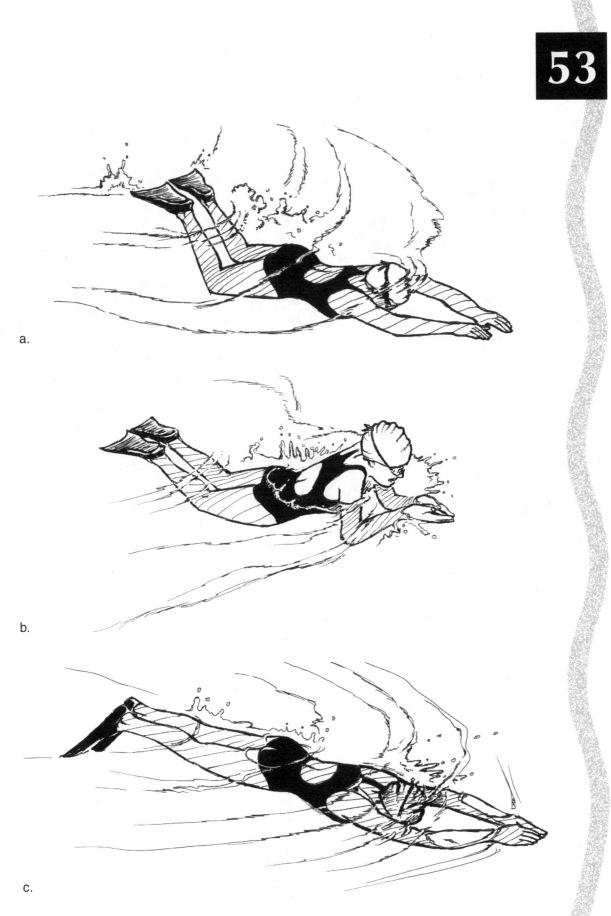

a.

b.

c.

Summer Sanders in the 1995 U.S. Open, © Dan Helms

CHAPTER SIX

Butterfly

When performed correctly, the butterfly is the most graceful and beautiful of all the strokes. Yet it is also the most difficult stroke for swimmers to master. It requires the most arm strength in order to lift the body above the surface, and the proper timing can require considerable practice.

The best butterflyers

- have excellent serpentine body action, and move through the water with a fluid wave action;

- have strong kicking, with the power generated from the hips;

- have good head position, looking primarily down and keeping the chin tucked in while breathing; and

- recover their arms with the elbows up and thumbs down.

The following drills will help swimmers achieve all of these fundamentals in their strokes in addition to excellent timing.

Butterfly Arm Action

Purpose

To teach proper mechanics of the armstroke, particularly the recovery and entry.

Description

The most common butterfly armstroke fault is the "hugging" recovery. This occurs when the arms recover with the thumbs turned upward and the palms facing forward—just like giving a hug. Recovering like this makes the stroke less effective. This drill works to eliminate that type of entry.

1. Lean forward a little, bending at the waist. Place your hands on your knees. Raise your arms so the backs of the hands (knuckle side) will be turned inward.

2. Simultaneously sweep both arms outward to about twice shoulder-width. Bend the elbows a little and rotate the hands inward to press back toward the waist. Continue to sweep the hands back, passing by the hips.

3. The arms will continue to press back until they are straight back, with the palms facing up. At this point, the hands should be as close together as possible.

4. The recovery phase begins by first relaxing the wrists and turning the arms so the wrists lead the motion, and the thumbs are pointing downward.

5. Keeping the elbows straight and the arms level, move the arms forward until they are directly in front of each shoulder. This completes the cycle.

Focus Points

- Maintain strength in the wrists during the pulling phase and keep them straight.
- Finish the pull with the palms facing up.
- Relax the wrists on the recovery.
- Let the wrists lead the recovery, with the thumbs pointing downward.

Tips

- Practice this slowly.
- Try practicing this in the water while standing up with your shoulders just above the surface.

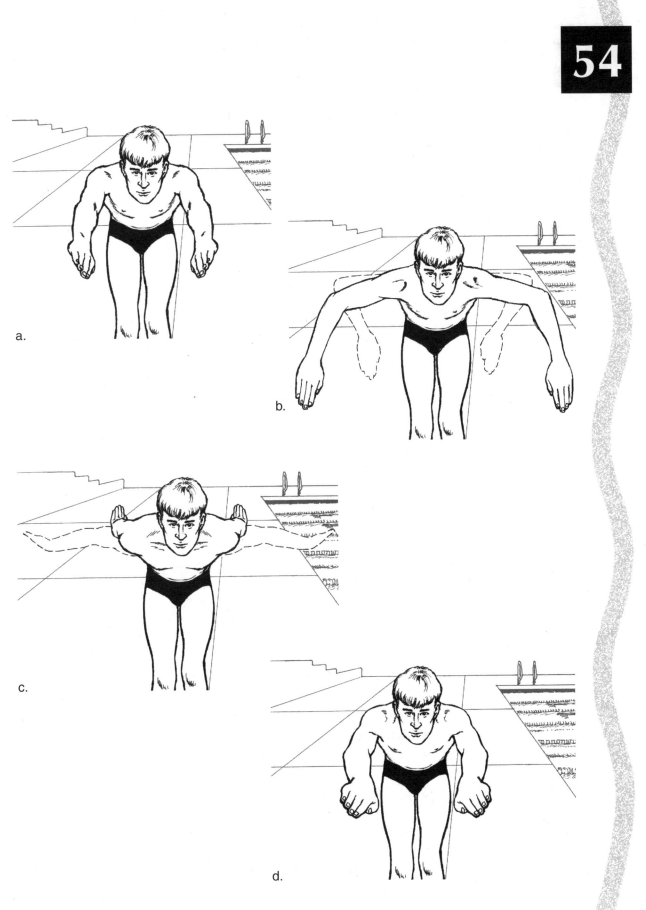

a.

b.

c.

d.

Dolphin Drill

Purpose

To teach the body action of the butterfly without the arm action. This is the first key drill in the butterfly series.

Description

1. During this drill, keep in mind the mermaid action of the butterfly kick—arms down at your sides, moving through the water in an "S" motion, your head leading the way as you propel through the water.

2. Put your fins on. Although your arms will stay down at your sides, it's OK if they scull a little when you breathe.

3. Begin by kicking three to four large dolphin kicks, staying about 2 feet underwater. Be sure to look down, not forward! Keep your head moving up and down at all times, flexing at the neck. The head action will start the kick, just like the handle of a whip.

4. Turn your head up to breathe. Do not kick as you breathe. As soon as your head breaks the surface, breathe quickly and then tuck your chin in so that your forehead enters the water first. This is called the dive.

5. As you dive, roll every part of your body above the surface in sequence—shoulders, hips, legs, and finally feet. As your feet re-enter the water, give a strong downward kick and do three or four large dolphin kicks underwater, then continue the cycle.

Focus Points

• Look down while kicking underwater.
• Keep your head moving.
• Get your forehead into the water first after breathing.
• After breathing, get your hips up above the surface.
• Remember the pattern: *breathe, dive, kick.*

Variations

• Perform this drill by going across the width of the pool, coming up and over loose lane ropes each time you breathe.

• For an advanced variation, perform this drill without going under the water, with the hips coming out high on each kick.

55

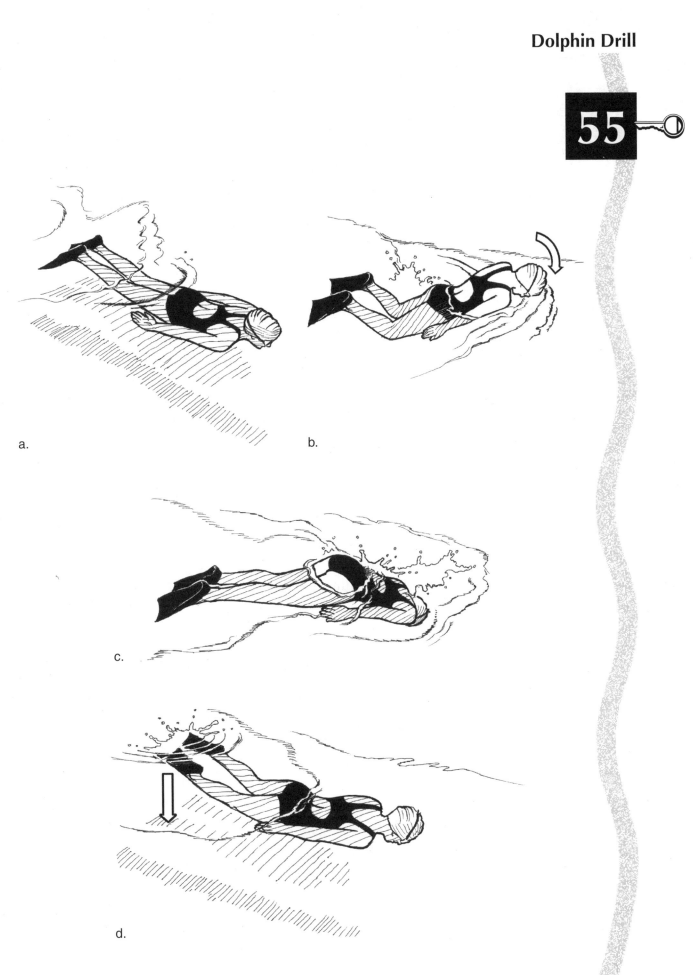

a.

b.

c.

d.

Dolphin Drill With Arms Extended

Purpose

To add the arm extension of the butterfly while continuing to practice the body action.

Description

1. This drill is performed exactly like Drill 55 (Dolphin Drill), except that your arms will now be out in front of you at all times.

2. Put your fins on. Lock your thumbs together and keep your arms stretched out in front of you while performing the body action in the previous drill. Be sure to look down while kicking under the water.

Focus Points

- Look down while kicking under the water.
- Keep your head moving.
- Get your forehead into the water first after breathing.
- After breathing, get the hips up high above the surface.
- Remember the pattern: *breathe, dive, kick*.

Tips

- Do not try to do this drill over the lane rope.
- For an advanced variation, perform this drill without going under the water, with your hips coming out high on each kick.

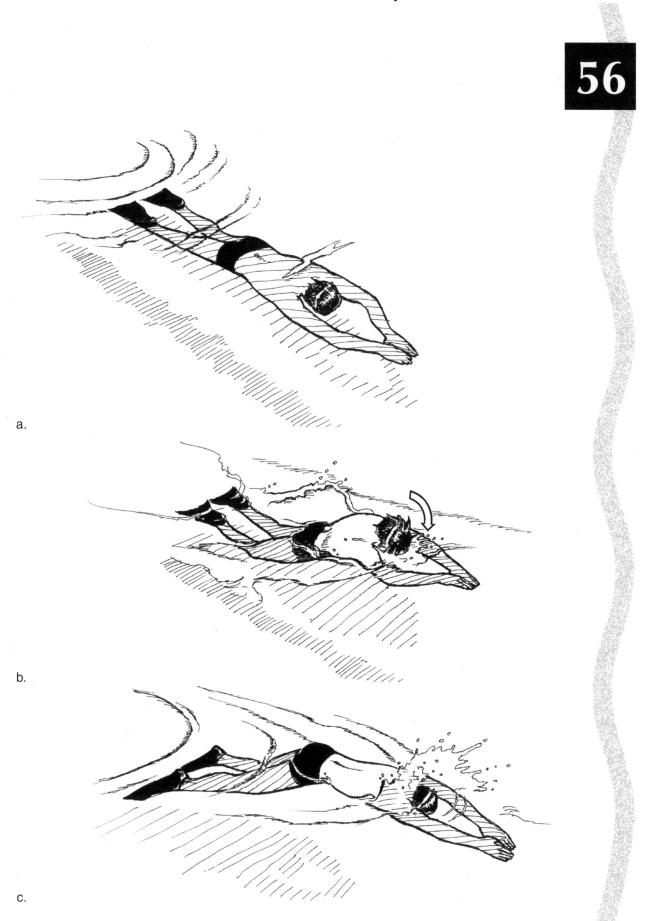

a.

b.

c.

Dolphin Drill With Arm Recovery

Purpose

To add the arm pull and recovery to the butterfly body action. This is the second key drill in the butterfly series.

Description

1. Put your fins on. This drill is the same as Drill 56 (Dolphin Drill With Arms Extended), except that in this drill you will pull your arms and take a single butterfly stroke when you come up to breathe. The sequence will now be *pull, breathe, dive, kick.*

2. As you pull with both arms, your body will lift. You should breathe when you reach the peak of your lift. As you finish the pull and begin the butterfly recovery with the arms, you will begin to return your head down into the water with the forehead entering first.

3. By the time you reach the dive, your arms will be back in front of you again with your head down. Lock the thumbs up again right away. Be sure to get the hips up.

4. Finish the stroke with a strong kick. Look down while kicking under the water.

Focus Points

- Remember the pattern: *pull, breathe, dive, kick.*
- Look down while kicking under the water.
- Get your forehead into the water first after breathing.
- After breathing, get your hips up above the surface.

Variations

- Perform this drill by going across the width of the pool over alternate loose lane ropes. Begin to pull just as you reach the lane rope. Do not touch the rope with your arms—swim over it. This is a fun drill that gives you good practice. Try to touch the lane rope as little as possible.

- For an advanced variation, perform this drill without going under the water, with your hips coming out high on each kick.

57

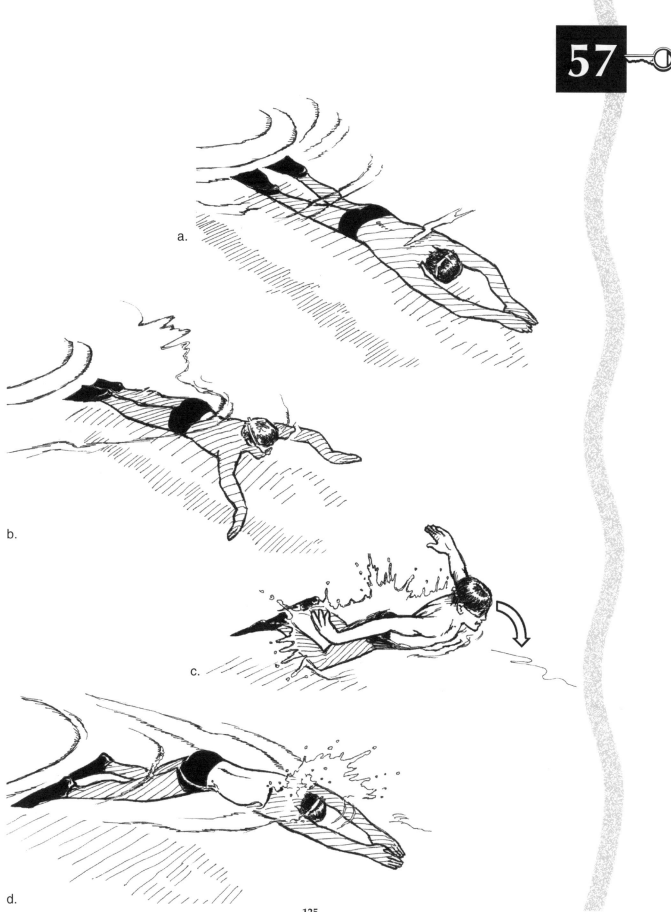

a.

b.

c.

d.

58

One-Arm Butterfly

Purpose

To transition to the continuous body action of the butterfly at the surface while gradually incorporating the arm action. This is the third key drill of the butterfly series.

Description

1. Put your fins on. You will keep one arm out in front of you at all times. Use the other arm to pull.

2. Stay on the surface and work on keeping the rhythm of *pull, breathe, dive, kick* in a continuous fashion.

3. Breathe to the side of the pulling arm. Briefly lock the thumbs each time you dive until you feel the kick.

4. Relax and go slowly. Look down when you dive. Be sure to get the hips up after breathing.

5. Repeat the cycle for the other arm.

Focus Points

- Maintain the rhythm: *pull, breathe, dive, kick.*
- Look down after you breathe.
- Get your hips up after breathing.
- Lock your thumbs each time until you feel the kick.

Variation

Alternate arms every lap, then every four strokes.

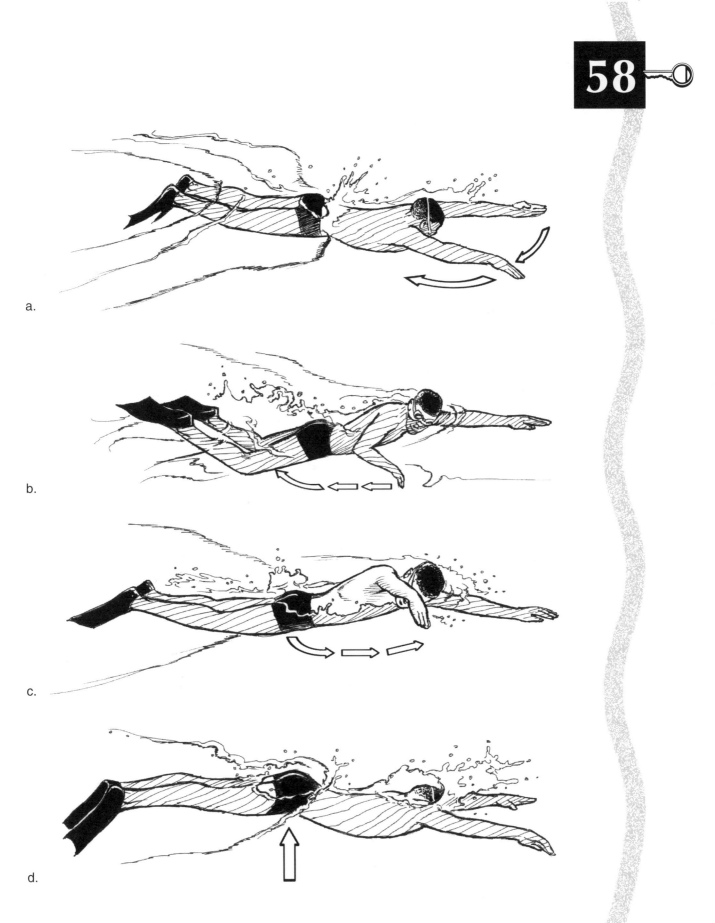

a.

b.

c.

d.

59

2 + 2 + 2

Purpose

To continue the transition to a complete butterfly, focusing on the body action. This is the fourth key drill in the butterfly series.

Description

1. Put your fins on. This drill combines the action of Drill 58 (One-Arm Butterfly) with the two-arm recovery.

2. Stay on the surface and concentrate on maintaining the rhythm of *pull, breathe, dive, kick* in a continuous fashion.

3. First, take two strokes (pull and recovery) with one arm, then two strokes with the other arm, and finally two strokes with both arms. Continue to repeat this cycle.

4. Try to breathe every other stroke. Breathe straight ahead when taking the two-arm stroke; breathe to the side when taking the one-arm stroke. Lock the thumbs up on each stroke when you dive until you feel the kick.

5. Relax and go slowly. Be sure to get the hips up on each stroke, as your hands come together in front.

Focus Points

- Concentrate on the rhythm: *pull, breathe, dive, kick.*
- Look down and get your hips up as your hands come together.
- Lock your thumbs up each time until you feel the kick.

Tip

See how slowly you can do this drill with control. Try to be very smooth.

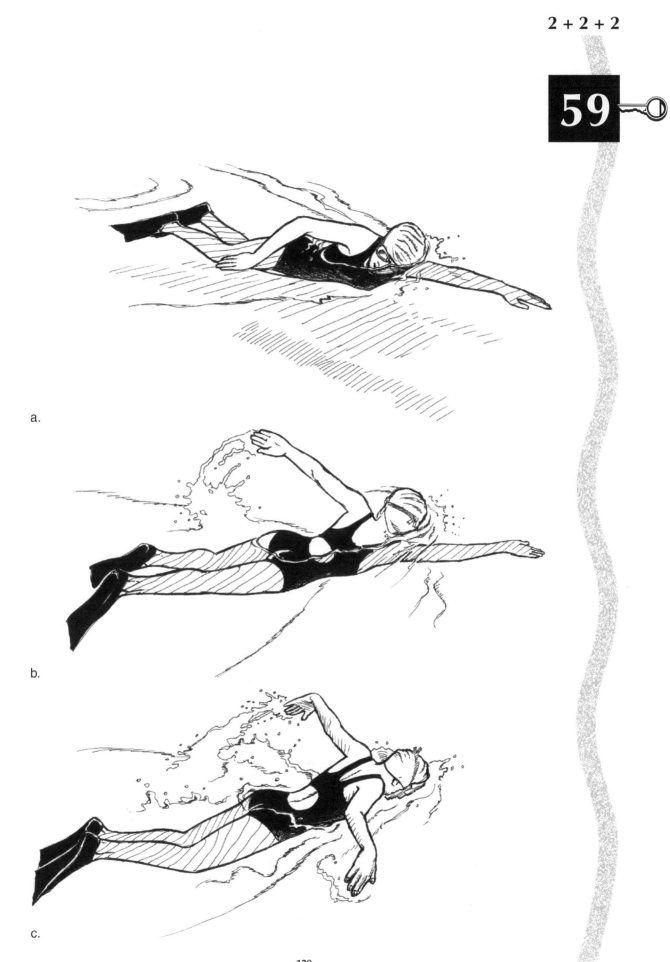

a.

b.

c.

60

Controlled Butterfly

Purpose

To complete the transition to a controlled butterfly. The emphasis remains on the body action. This is the fifth key drill in the butterfly series.

Description

1. Put your fins on. This drill simply eliminates the one-arm action of the previous drill; use both arms for every stroke. Stay on the surface and work on keeping the rhythm of *pull, breathe, dive, kick* in a continuous fashion.

2. Try to breathe every other stroke. Lock your thumbs up briefly on each stroke when you dive. Relax and go slowly. Be sure to get your hips up on each stroke as your hands come together.

3. As you become stronger, another rhythm cycle that you can use is simply *reach, kick*. As your arms enter the water, that is the reach. As the feet kick down, that is the kick. The timing between the reach and kick should be very even.

Focus Points

- Keep a nice flowing rhythm: *pull, breathe, dive, kick.*
- Eventually use this rhythm: *reach, kick.*
- Look down after each breath.
- Get your hips up on each stroke.
- Lock your thumbs on each stroke until you feel the kick.

Tip

Stay nice and relaxed. Let the stroke technique do the work for you. You may notice that as you swim a little faster, a second kick in the middle of each stroke will usually occur naturally. However, in doing this drill, you don't need to focus on the second kick. For most, this second kick is a minor kick that gives balance to the rhythm of the stroke. For some, the second kick can become very strong. It is usually best to first focus on a nice fluid motion.

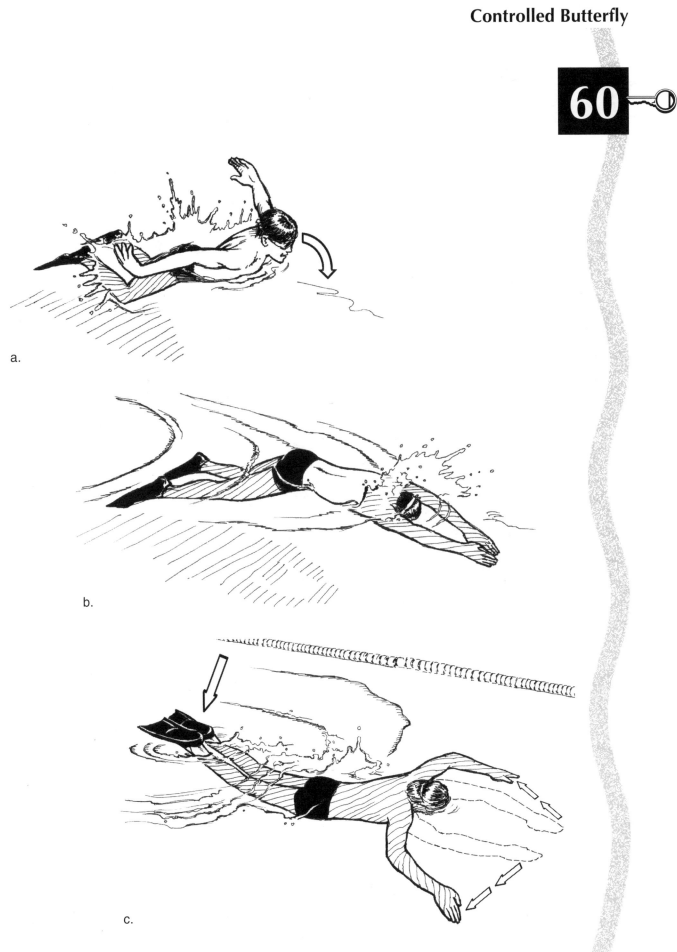

a.

b.

c.

Summer Sanders in the 1992 Mission Viejo Invitational, © Dan Helms

CHAPTER SEVEN

Freestyle and Backstroke Turns

Approximately one-quarter of the race involves starts, turns, and finishes. These maneuvers require skill, precision, and speed. Even small errors in execution can easily separate the champion from the average swimmer. Swimmers must consistently practice good starts, turns, and finishes.

These drills teach you how to

- perform a proper flip (somersault) for both the freestyle and backstroke turns;
- control your breathing while approaching the wall on the freestyle turn;
- approach the wall smoothly and accurately for the backstroke turn; and
- land your feet properly at the wall and push off to a streamline position.

This chapter will address the most frequently performed turn—the freestyle turn, as well as the most troublesome turn—the backstroke turn. The following drills provide a systematic approach to mastering the fundamentals of these turns.

61

Streamline and Somersault

Purpose

The somersault is the first step in learning how to perform a proper flip turn for both the freestyle and backstroke turns. If the somersault cannot be performed in the water, practice on a padded surface such as a mattress.

Description

1. Push off the wall on your front into a streamline position at the surface of the water. Keep your face in the water and blow bubbles.

2. Hold the streamline for a count of three. Bend at the waist, then drive the head down and back toward your knees. At the same time, extend your arms out away from your body and scull in a circular motion to help you spin faster. Your knees should be bent. You should perform a very fast somersault in a fairly tight tuck position. Do the somersault as high as possible with your body traveling mostly through the air rather than the water.

3. When you finish the somersault, come up right away and check to see if you are facing the same direction as when you started. Return to the wall and repeat as necessary.

Focus Points

- Absolutely do not breathe until after you complete the somersault.
- Drive your head down quickly as you go into the somersault.
- Use your arms to help you spin faster and to stay straight.
- Keep your body high as you flip.

Variation

For an advanced variation, as you gain more strength and speed, try to let your feet travel a greater distance through the air. As a result, you will not have such a tight tuck when you flip but will achieve more of a layout position.

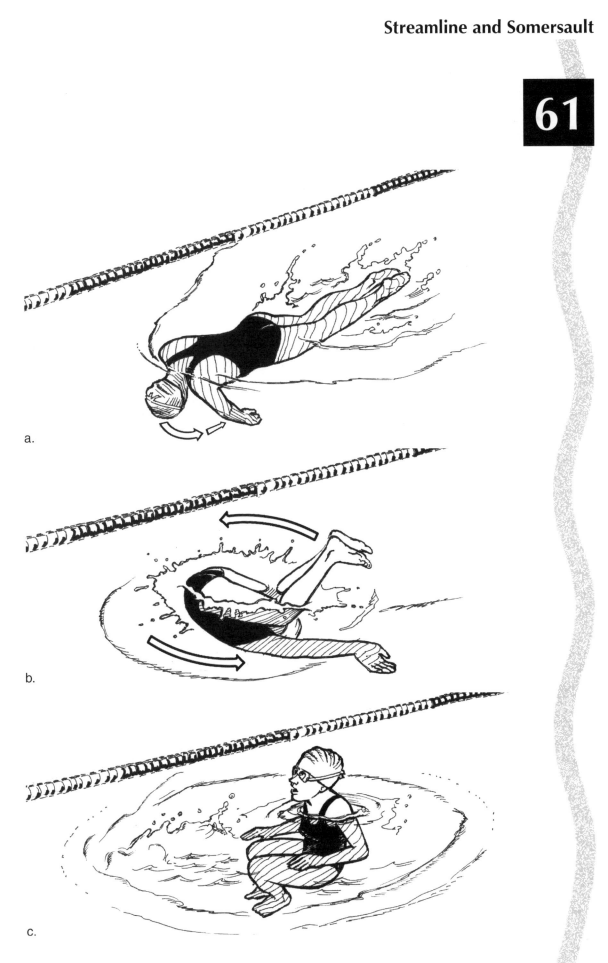

a.

b.

c.

Swim and Somersault

Purpose

This is the second step for the flip turns. The focus in this drill is on controlling the breathing while going into the turn and on immediately pulling through the flip.

Description

1. Swim three freestyle strokes without breathing.
2. Then, without any hesitation, pull down with just one arm and go into a quick somersault.
3. After completing the somersault, pause to breathe.
4. Continue to repeat this cycle down the lane.

Focus Points

- Control your breathing for the three strokes and the somersault.
- Do not hesitate or pause as you go into the flip.
- Pull through the somersault with one arm. Avoid having both your hands down at your sides before going into the somersault.
- Drive your head quickly into the flip.
- Keep your body high.

Variation

Try to pull through the somersault with either arm.

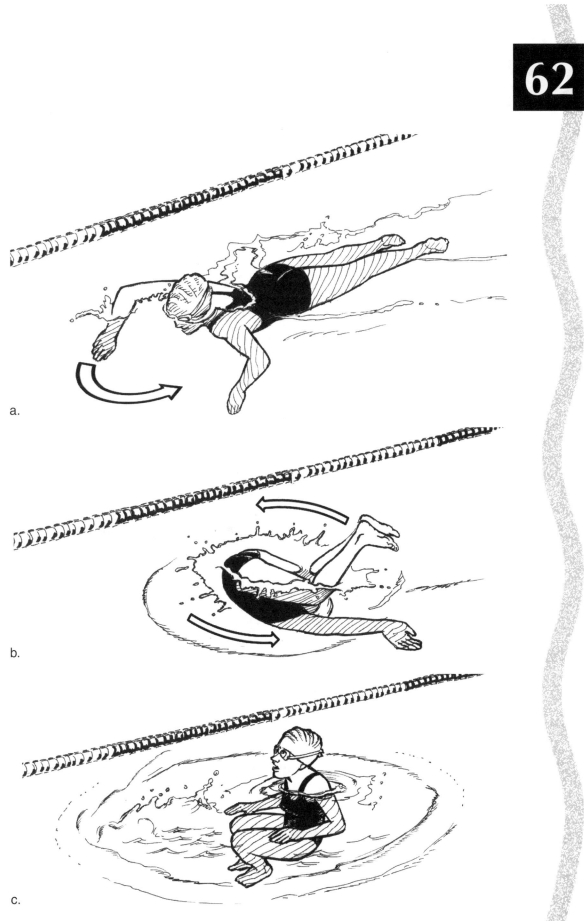

a.

b.

c.

63

Foot Touch

Purpose

This is the third step for the flip turns. This drill will reinforce the breathing control on the approach, and teach the landing of the feet at the wall accurately.

Description

1. Begin about 10 to 12 yards away from the wall. Swim freestyle toward the wall. Control your breathing from the flags (5 yards) on in.

2. When you are at least two strokes away from the wall, perform your somersault, having your feet land on the wall about 1 foot below the surface. If you are too far away, continue to repeat the approach and gradually turn closer to the wall until you find the right distance for your turn.

3. Do not push off; just land your feet. You should be able to look at your feet while underwater to see where they land on the wall.

4. When your feet land properly on the wall, your body will be in a "lounge chair" position underwater (on your back with the hips and knees slightly bent), and your hands will be just above your head. Your feet will land about 1 to 2 feet deep, depending on your size. (If you are smaller, your feet will be higher; if you are bigger, your feet will be lower.)

Focus Points

- Control your breathing so you can focus on the wall.
- Perform a quick, high flip.
- Look to see where your feet land.

Tip

Master the ability to pull through the turn with either arm.

a.

b.

c.

64

Streamline Pushoff

Purpose

This is the fourth step for the flip turns. This drill will focus on achieving a proper streamline along with control of depth and sufficient distance. Pushing off from the turns and achieving almost no streamline is a common error.

Description

1. Begin by facing the wall. Hold onto the gutter wall with your hands and place the balls of your feet on the wall about 1 to 2 feet deep. (Depth depends on the size of the swimmer.)
2. Lower your head *under* the water.
3. Let go of the wall with your *hands* and place them just above your head.
4. *Push* off the wall.
5. As you leave the wall, you should reach a tight *streamline* position.
6. Streamline about 1 to 2 feet deep so that you gradually come to the surface, at least past the flags. Once you have control of the depth with just the streamline, add flutter kicking and try to travel farther on your streamline.

Focus Points

- Follow steps 2 through 5 precisely!
- Control the depth so that you are neither too deep nor too shallow.
- Focus on the pattern *under, hands, push, streamline.*

Tip

Combine the practice of this drill with Drill 63 (Foot Touch). First do the foot touch and stop; then do the streamline pushoff. Continue to repeat this cycle.

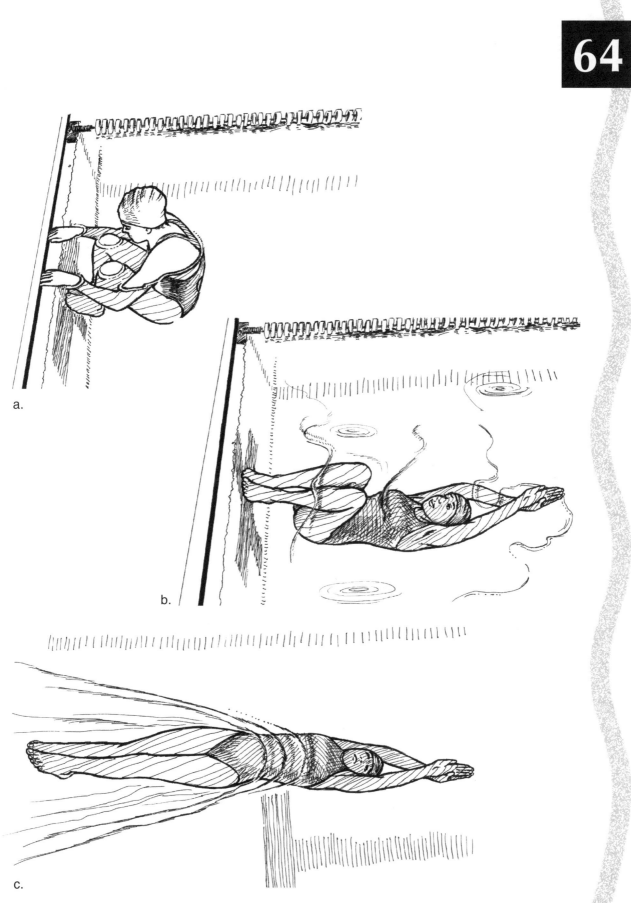

a.

b.

c.

65

Backstroke Breakout

Purpose

This fifth step for the flip turns will teach the proper method of beginning the backstroke either from a start or after a turn.

Description

1. Start by pushing off the wall just as you did in Drill 64 (Streamline Pushoff). As you clear the wall, begin a flutter kick.

2. Kick for a count of at least four and then pull one arm down to your side to begin the backstroke arm action.

3. Control your depth so that you break the surface just as you finish your first arm pull.

4. Complete about three strokes.

Focus Points

- Control your depth.
- Hold a tight streamline for a count of four or more.
- Pull only one arm down first before starting your backstroke.

Variation

Once you master this drill with the flutter kick, you can add dolphin kicking in the streamline position and try to get a lot more distance and speed (depending on the individual). However, be sure to control your depth. The dolphin kick is used mostly with the backstroke start, but is also effective for some swimmers in the freestyle pushoff.

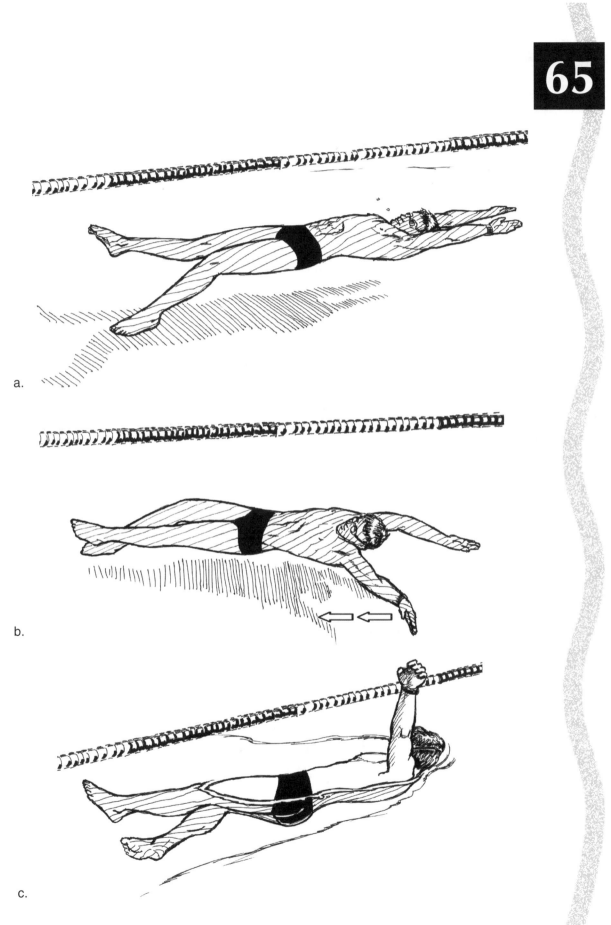

a.

b.

c.

66

Freestyle-to-Backstroke Turn

Purpose

The sixth step for the flip turn is a key drill that should be practiced frequently. It allows the swimmer to focus on the proper mechanics of the turn and work on achieving the greatest speed possible.

Description

Now you will combine Drills 63 (Foot Touch) and 65 (Backstroke Breakout). This will become a freestyle-to-backstroke turn. This is a very important drill because it will help you learn to control your approach, pushoff, and eventually speed. Practice doing this correctly several times before you try to increase your speed.

1. Swim freestyle to the wall with the proper breath control.
2. Then perform your flip and land your feet on the wall, just as in the foot touch drill.
3. Then, push off underwater into the streamline position and start your backstroke breakout.
4. Practice being accurate first. Look to see where you land before you push off. Keep the turn under control.

Focus Point

Be in control. Don't rush it.

Tip

Once you master the mechanics of this drill and consistently place your landing correctly, try to anticipate the wall and begin to push off just before your feet land. This way you will bounce off the wall very quickly. This will help you develop the fastest turn possible.

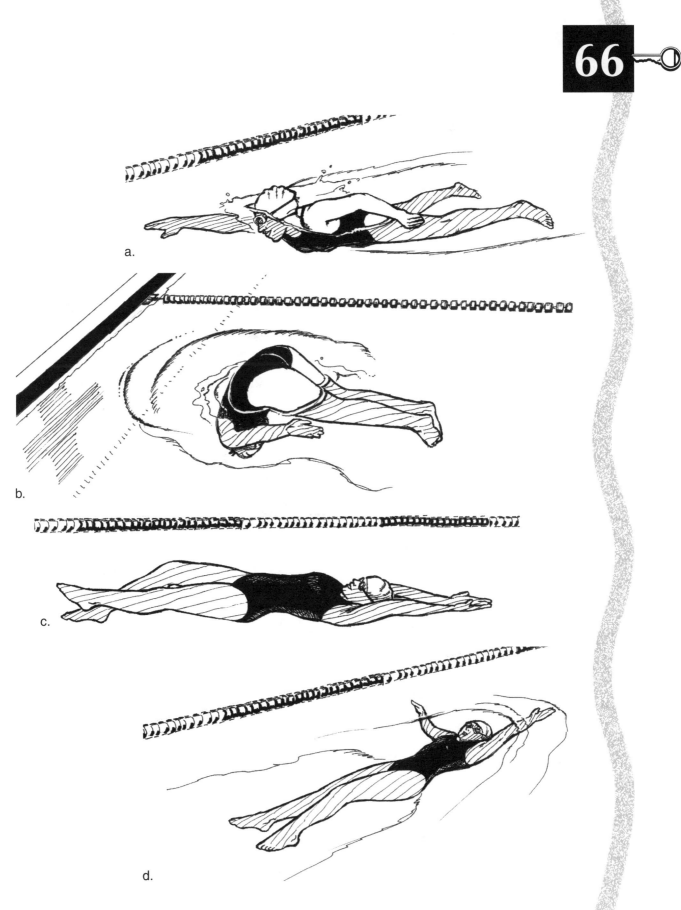

a.

b.

c.

d.

Backstroke Finish

Purpose

To teach swimmers a safe method to determine the stroke count from the flags to the wall for the backstroke. This stroke count is important for both the finish and the turn.

Description

1. Start at the middle of the pool. Swim backstroke full speed toward the wall.

2. Just as you pass directly underneath the backstroke flags, begin to count your strokes. At first, take just two strokes past the flags and then kick in the rest of the way, with your arm overhead.

3. Finish by letting your hand touch the wall with your fingers pointing down. Bend the elbow of the up arm just a little as you kick in on your last stroke. You should not have to look back for the wall at all. Just focus on the flags and your stroke count.

4. If you have room, add one more stroke the next time. As long as you have room remaining, continue to add one stroke at a time until you reach a safe number of strokes.

5. Be consistent in how you count the number of strokes you take from the flags. Ideally, on your last stroke, your hand will enter the water between 1 and 3 feet away from the wall. This will be a safe finish.

Focus Points

- Practice this drill at full speed.
- Kick in hard.
- Focus on the flags, not the wall.
- Be consistent in how you count your strokes.
- Know your stroke count!

Tip

It is better to take fewer, more powerful strokes with lots of strong kicking than a greater number of choppy, short strokes. Try to establish the lowest number of strokes with great speed and complete safety.

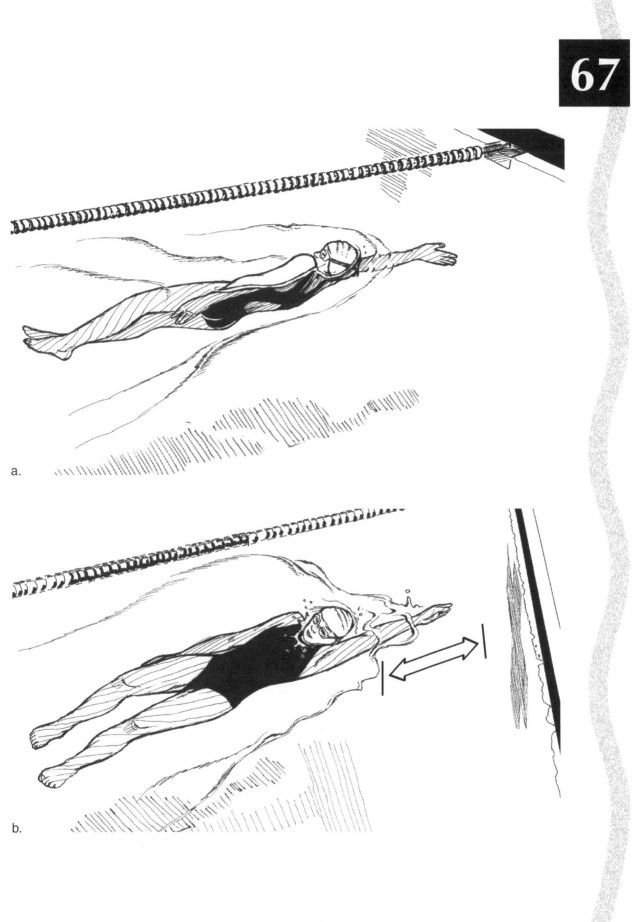

a.

b.

68

Corkscrew Swimming

Purpose

To practice rolling properly onto the stomach before performing the backstroke flip turn.

Description

1. This is called corkscrew swimming, because you will twist and spiral through the water just like a corkscrew through a cork. Start by swimming one armstroke of freestyle on your front. Turn your head to breathe, and keep turning your head and body so that you are on your back. Then recover the down arm using a backstroke recovery, and pull with the up arm. Continue to turn your head and body in the same direction until you are completely on your front side. This completes one corkscrew stroke. Flutter kick throughout.

2. Taking very smooth and controlled strokes, swim the corkscrew stroke in one direction for four strokes, and then swim the corkscrew stroke in the other direction. Repeat this several times.

Focus Points

- Keep the stroke smooth.
- Keep a steady kick.

Tip

See how few corkscrew strokes you can take per lap. The fewer the better.

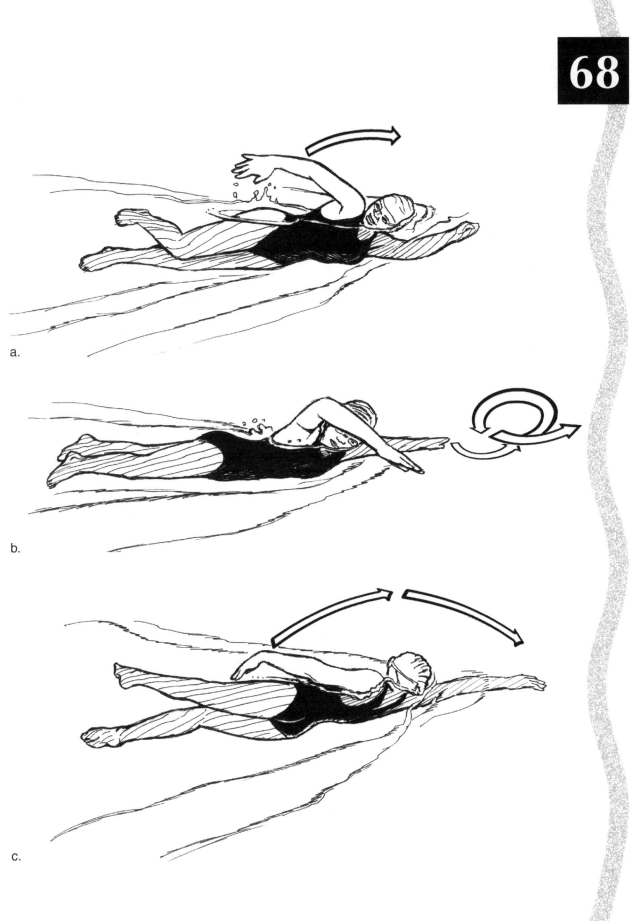

a.

b.

c.

69

Backstroke Turn

Purpose

To complete the process for the backstroke turn.

Description

Now you will be able to complete the backstroke turn. Remember what your stroke count is for the backstroke finish, but note that you might need to make a minor adjustment to the number of strokes you take for the turn.

1. Subtract one from your stroke count for the backstroke finish (Drill 67). This will be the number of backstroke arm strokes you will take from the flags.

2. After your arm enters the water for the last armstroke, you will then roll to that same side. Then, with the other arm, take one corkscrew stroke (freestyle recovery) to get to your stomach.

3. Then you will be in position to do your flip, just as in Drill 66 (Freestyle-to-Backstroke Turn). The total number of strokes for your turn should be the same as for your finish.

4. Practice this first in the open water before trying it at the wall. Keep the strokes smooth.

5. If you find that you are consistently too far away from the wall, you may need to add a stroke. If you find that you are consistently too close, you should subtract a stroke. Once you push off, complete the backstroke breakout.

Focus Points

- Keep a steady stroke rhythm.
- Keep a strong kick.
- Focus on consistency.

Tip

Roll very smoothly and gradually. Remember that the action must be continuous once your shoulders are past the vertical position.

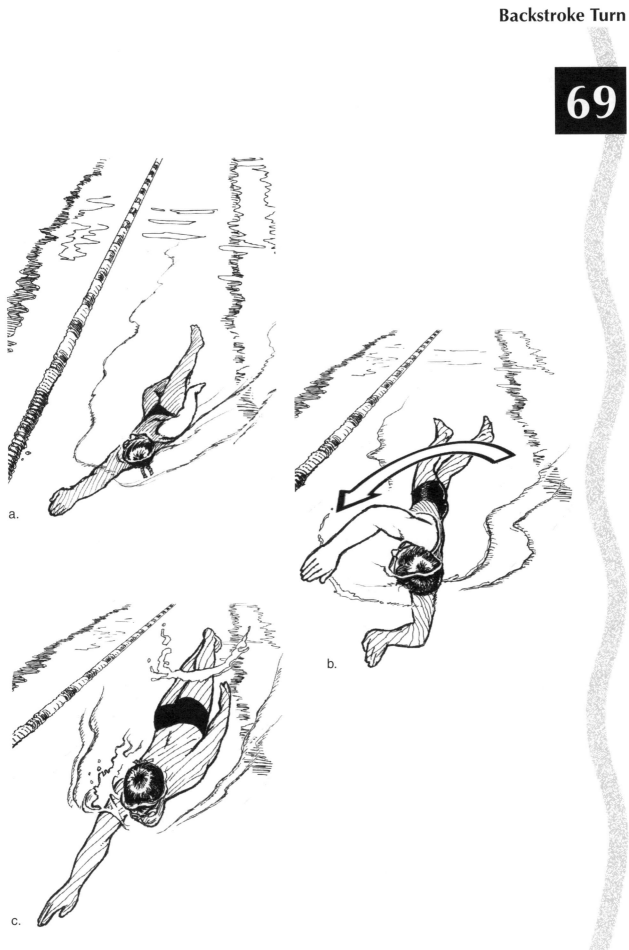

a.

b.

c.

70

Freestyle Turn

Purpose

To complete the process for the freestyle turn.

Description

It is important to realize that the rules do not require that a swimmer be on his front side when he leaves the wall. Since twisting on the wall slows the turn, this drill will focus on rotating the body *after* the pushoff from the wall, during the streamline portion of the turn.

1. Review Drill 66 (Freestyle-to-Backstroke Turn).
2. Swim freestyle to the wall with proper breath control.
3. Then perform your flip, and land your feet on the wall.
4. Next, push off underwater into a streamline position on your back.
5. Just *after* you push off the wall on your back, you will begin to roll to your side while kicking in the streamline position.
6. Do not twist on the wall. Gradually and smoothly rotate your body while you are kicking in the streamline.
7. Once you count to four, begin to pull your arm down and continue to roll to your freestyle position. Then begin swimming freestyle.

Focus Points

- Push off while still on your back.
- Rotate your body after you clear the wall, not while on the wall.
- Rotate gradually and smoothly.

Tips

- Focus on the mechanics first before trying to increase your speed.
- Try to control your breathing for the first two to three strokes after your turn.

a.

b.

c.

d.

CHAPTER EIGHT

Other Turns and Finishes

Four of the seven turns in competitive swimming require a simultaneous two-hand touch at the wall, followed by the turning of the body and pushing off into the next segment of the race. Many swimmers have difficulty making these turns in a smooth manner because of their complexity. Specific skills are required in order to make these turns quickly and efficiently. The mastery of certain details and/or the correction of faults can make a significant difference. This chapter addresses the basic mechanics necessary to make these turns effectively, then covers each one specifically.

These drills will focus on

- touching and releasing quickly from the wall;
- developing the proper sequence of steps in making an effective turn;
- attaining a streamline position off the wall; and
- finishing into the wall or touch pad in a streamline position.

This chapter also addresses the backstroke-to-breaststroke turn, which only requires a one-hand touch. While considerable variation is possible in the execution of this turn, a basic style is presented. Once this approach is mastered, more advanced styles can then be considered.

71

Two-Hand Touch Turn

Purpose

To understand the basic mechanics for the two-hand touch turn. This applies to four turns: butterfly-to-butterfly, butterfly-to-backstroke, breaststroke-to-breaststroke, and breaststroke-to-freestyle.

Description

All of these turns require you to roll a little to the side once you have touched the wall with both hands together. You should never release both hands from the wall at the same time. You should have a two-step release of the hands. The first hand to release goes underwater, the second hand to release travels over the water. Follow these steps:

1. *Touch* the wall with both hands, bring your knees in under your chest, and place your feet on the wall.
2. With one arm, pull an imaginary ripcord from the wall and *turn* to the side. Roll the same shoulder back.
3. Push your head *under*water.
4. *Throw* the trail arm past your head so that your hands come together.
5. *Push* off underwater and streamline.

Focus Points

- Practice the steps slowly and in order.
- On the butterfly-to-backstroke turn, you will drive the arm back directly over your head. On the other turns, you will *throw* more to the side and in front of your face, similar to a freestyle recovery.
- Remember the pattern: *touch, turn, under, throw, push*.

Tip

As you increase speed, try to release the first hand as quickly as possible.

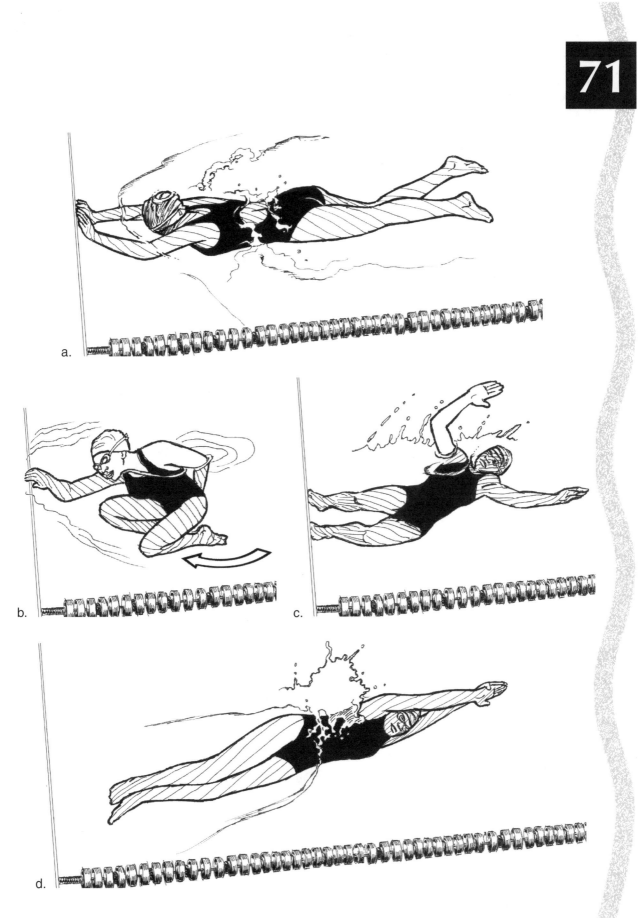

a.

b.

c.

d.

Breaststroke Finish

Purpose

To finish the breaststroke properly.

Description

The most common error is for swimmers to shorten their strokes as they approach the wall, and take more strokes instead of fewer strokes and a strong kick and glide into the wall.

1. Start from 10 to 12 yards away from the wall. Swim breaststroke at full speed toward the wall. When you reach the flags, try to take fewer strokes to the wall.
2. On the last stroke, get your arms completely stretched out in front of you in a streamline position as you kick and glide into the wall.
3. Drive your head down into the streamline as you finish into the wall. Your fingertips should touch the wall underwater.
4. Remember that your hands must touch the wall at the same time. Otherwise, you could be disqualified from a race.

Focus Points

- Finish in a streamline.
- Touch the wall underwater.

Tips

- Practice the breaststroke kick underwater while holding a streamline position with your arms. See how far you can glide for each kick.
- Practice kicking into the wall underwater from about 5 to 10 yards away. Get a feel for how much distance you can cover with each kick.

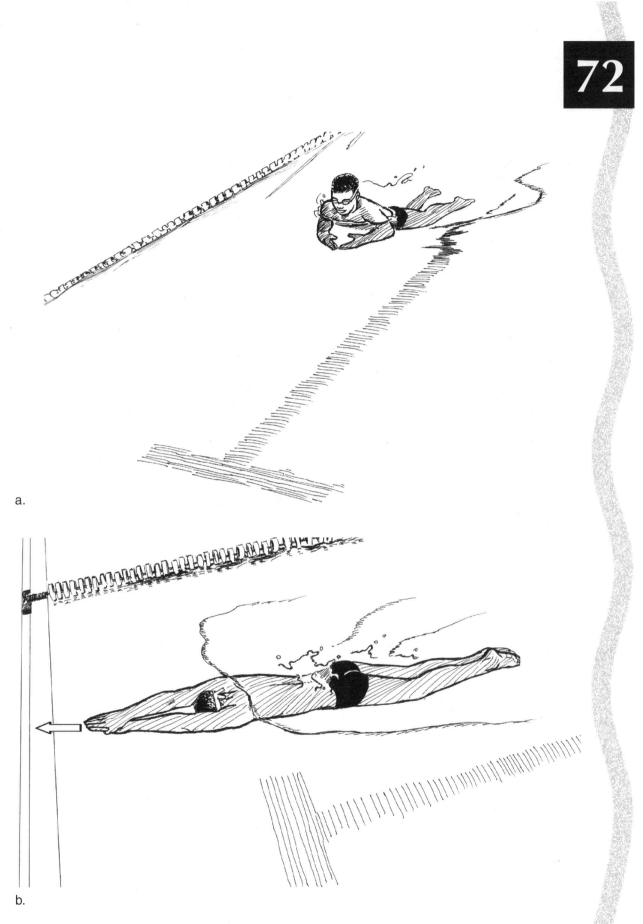

a.

b.

Breaststroke Pullout

Purpose

To perform a proper breaststroke pullout for the starts and turns. This instruction will give a general guide for good timing in the sequence. A well-executed pullout is a distinct advantage in a race.

Description

1. Push off the wall on your stomach, underwater, into a streamline position, facing down toward the bottom. Hold this position for a count of three.

2. Pull your arms down underneath you, until your hands finish on your legs just above your knees. Pull deeply, with your fingers pointing downward. Hold the finish position for a count of two. You should still be facing down.

3. Bring your hands up to your stomach and bring your heels in to prepare for the breaststroke kick.

4. Kick your legs and extend your arms directly forward into a streamline position.

5. Hold the streamline position for a count of one.

6. Begin your breaststroke.

Focus Points

- Remember this pattern of gliding: *three, two, one.*
- Practice all the steps.
- Maintain consistent depth.

Tips

- There are several steps to this turn. Practice by adding one step at a time.
- For an advanced variation, see how far you can travel underwater when you perform this correctly.

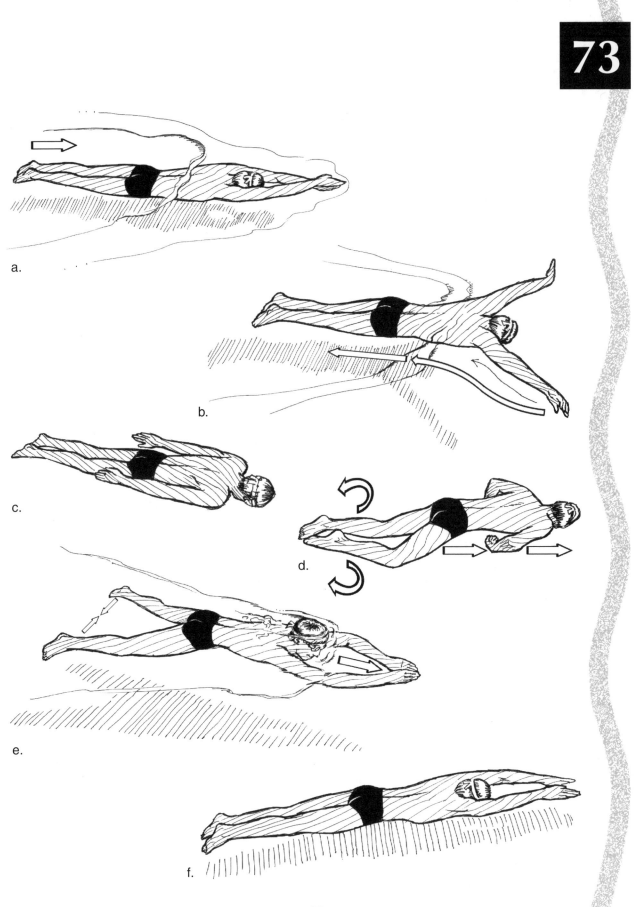

a.

b.

c.

d.

e.

f.

74

Breaststroke Turn

Purpose

To perform a proper breaststroke turn. This is a matter of putting together three parts—the approach, turn, and pull-out.

Description

1. Approach the wall swimming the breaststroke.

2. Unlike the finish, let your hands touch next to each other on the wall or on the gutter.

3. Perform the two-hand touch turn. Remember the pattern: *touch, turn, under, throw, push.*

4. Hold the streamline position for a count of three and continue the rest of the pullout.

Focus Points

- Keep your head low on the turn.
- Be sure that your shoulders are level before you do the pulldown. Otherwise it is illegal.

Tip

Bring your knees in as fast as you can once you touch. This will give you a faster turn.

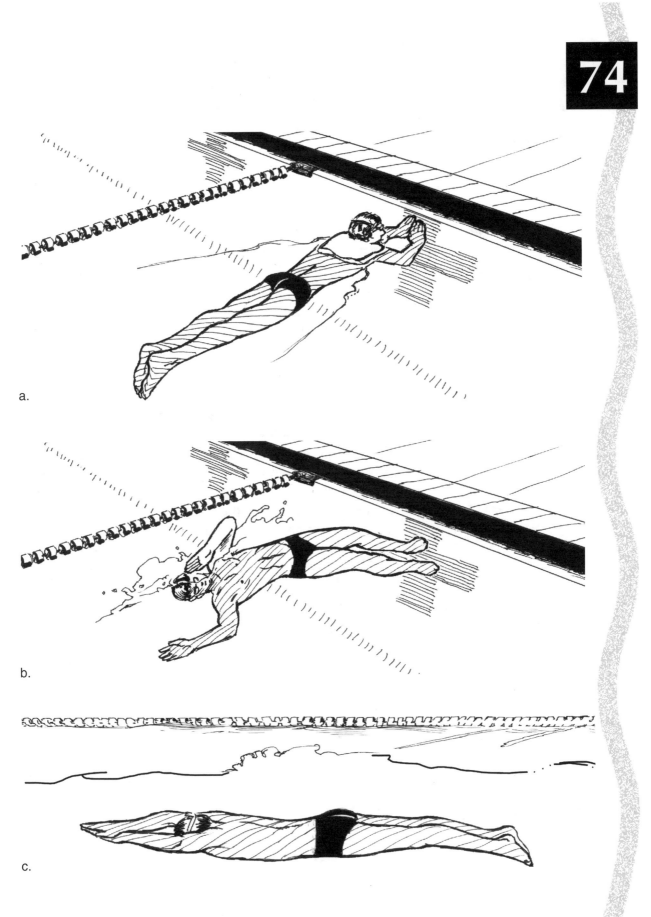

a.

b.

c.

75

Butterfly Finish

Purpose

To perform a proper finish for the butterfly.

Description

Swimmers commonly shorten their strokes as they approach the wall, but it is faster to take fewer strokes and kick in while holding a streamline position rather than take short, choppy strokes to the wall.

1. Start from 10 to 12 yards away from the wall.

2. Swim the butterfly at full speed toward the wall. Once you get to the flags, try to take fewer strokes to the wall and control your breathing.

3. On your last stroke, get your arms completely stretched out in front of you in a streamline position as you dolphin kick to the wall.

4. Drive your head down into the streamline as you finish to the wall. Your fingertips should touch the wall underwater. Remember, the hands must touch at the same time. Otherwise, you could be disqualified from a race.

Focus Points

- Finish in a streamline position.
- If you are a little too far to touch right away, kick in.
- Touch underwater.
- Try to take the fewest number of strokes possible for the finish.

Tip

If you have to kick in, accelerate your kick to hyperspeed; make it very quick.

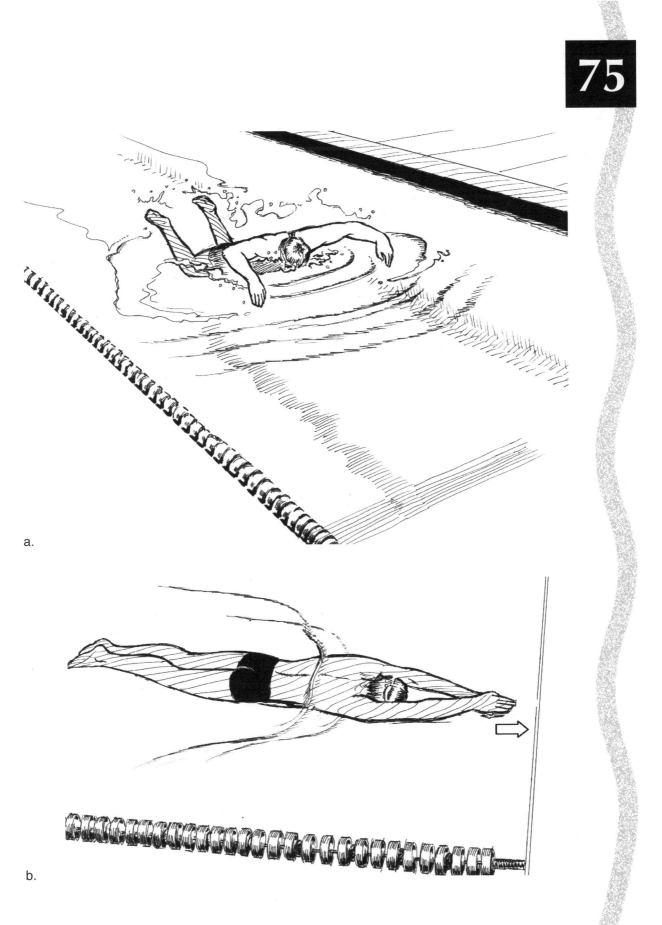

a.

b.

Butterfly Breakout

Purpose

To perform a proper butterfly breakout for the starts and turns.

Description

One problem is that swimmers often fail to streamline and dolphin kick underwater for a sufficient distance.

1. Start from the wall. Push off in a streamline position and be sure to control your depth.
2. As soon as you reach the fully extended streamline, begin to dolphin kick at a very quick pace.
3. Get in at least three to four kicks before beginning your pulling action to start the stroke.
4. Control your depth so that you break the surface just as you are finishing the pulling on the first stroke. Also, control your breathing for the first two to three strokes.

Focus Points

- Keep a tight streamline.
- Maintain quick kicking.
- Travel 5 to 10 yards underwater as quickly as you can.

Tip

Practice dolphin kicking underwater in a streamline as far as you can go. This will help to build up your breath control during the breakout.

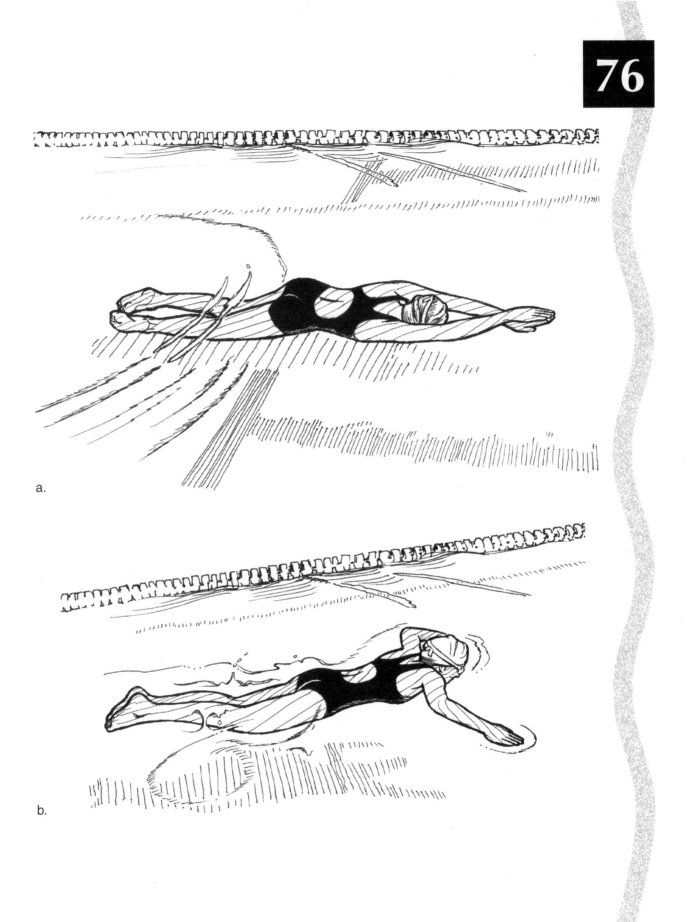

a.

b.

Butterfly Turn

Purpose

To perform a proper butterfly turn. This is a matter of putting together three parts—the approach, turn, and breakout.

Description

1. Start 10 to 12 yards away from the wall. Swim the butterfly at full speed toward the wall.
2. Unlike the finish, let your hands touch next to each other on the wall or on the gutter.
3. Perform the two-hand touch turn. Remember the pattern: *touch, turn, under, throw, push.*
4. Get into the streamline position and perform the breakout.

Focus Points

- Keep your head low on the turn.
- Be sure that your shoulders are level before you do the pulldown on your first stroke. Otherwise, it is illegal.

Tip

Bring the knees in as fast as you can once you touch the wall. This will give you a faster turn.

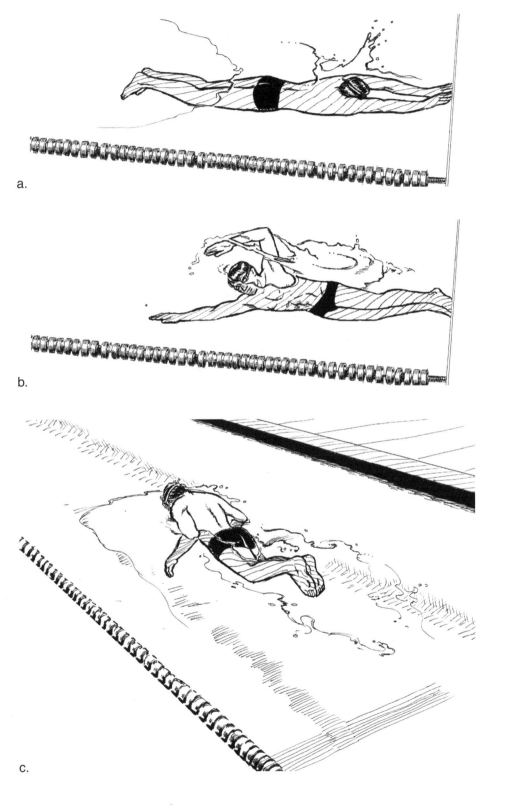

a.

b.

c.

78

Butterfly-to-Backstroke Turn

Purpose

To perform a proper butterfly-to-backstroke turn.

Description

The most common error in the butterfly-to-backstroke turn is releasing both hands from the wall at the same time. The mechanics for the turn are the same as the other two-hand touch turns.

1. Start 10 to 12 yards away from the wall. Swim the butterfly at full speed toward the wall.
2. Let your hands touch next to each other on the wall or on the gutter.
3. Perform the two-hand touch turn. Remember the pattern: *touch, turn, under, throw, push.* (But this time remember to *throw* directly overhead.) On this turn, the feet will not need to twist on the wall, just the shoulders.
4. Get into the streamline position and perform the backstroke breakout.

Focus Points

- Keep your head low on the turn.
- Lean your head straight back after the touch.
- Roll your shoulders so that you push off a little on your side.
- Drive the arm back directly over your head.

Tips

- Bring your knees in as fast as you can once you touch. This will give you a faster turn.
- Watch your hand release from the wall and drive over your head.

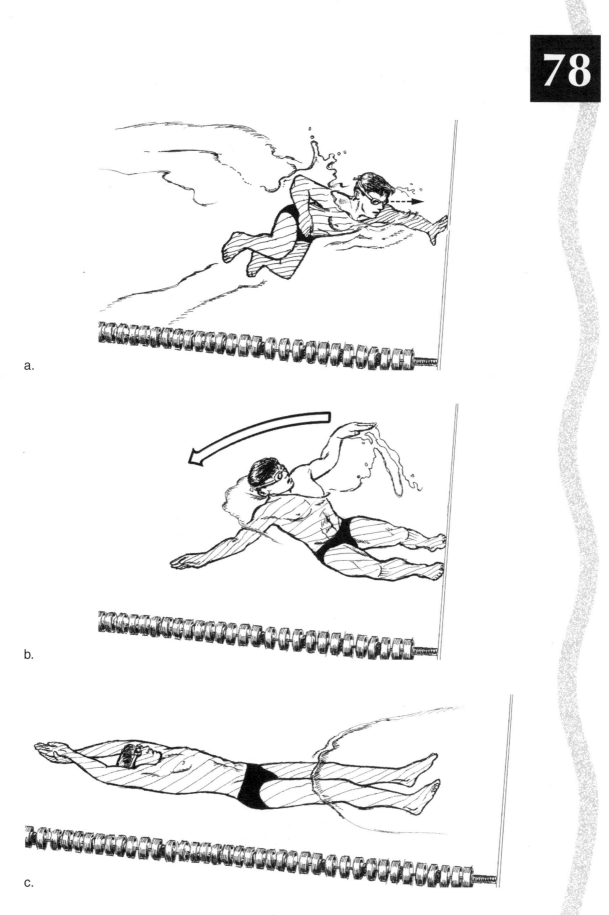

a.

b.

c.

79

Backstroke-to-Breaststroke Turn

Purpose

To perform a proper backstroke-to-breaststroke turn.

Description

There are several variations of the backstroke-to-breaststroke turn. The open turn, described below, is the simplest, and is quite effective. An advanced version, the backstroke-to-breaststroke flip turn, if executed properly, can be a remarkably fast turn. However, a well-executed open turn will serve the swimmer well.

1. Start 10 to 12 yards away from the wall. Swim the backstroke at full speed toward the wall.

2. If there is a gutter, rotate your hand on the final stroke so that your palm is face down and your thumb extends downward. The fingers will then slide over the gutter wall.

3. Grab the wall with one hand and pull your feet in underneath you so you can place your feet on the wall.

4. You can then drop your head underwater, throw your arm, and streamline into your breaststroke pullout.

5. If there is no gutter, position your hand on the final stroke so that your fingers are pointing to the opposite side and your thumb is pointing up. Use your hand to push away from the wall as you position your body for the pushoff.

Focus Points

- Keep your head low on the turn.
- Use just one arm to perform the turn.

Tips

- Bring your knees in as fast as you can once you touch. This will give you a faster turn.
- Try not to twist too much on the wall. It is all right to be a little on your side; in fact, it is a lot faster. Just remember that your shoulders have to be level by the time you do your pulldown.

a.

b.

Breaststroke-to-Freestyle Turn

Purpose

To perform a proper breaststroke-to-freestyle turn.

Description

1. Start 10 to 12 yards away from the wall. Swim the breaststroke at full speed toward the wall.
2. Let your hands touch next to each other on the wall or on the gutter.
3. Perform the two-hand touch turn. Remember the pattern: *touch, turn, under, throw, push.* Try to push off mostly on your side.
4. Get into the streamline position and do the freestyle breakout. Control your breathing for at least two strokes.

Focus Points

- Keep your head low on the turn.
- Control your breathing for the first two strokes of the freestyle.

Tips

- Bring your knees in as fast as you can once you touch. This will give you a faster turn.
- The most common error for this turn is no streamline. This turn starts the final leg of the individual medley when most swimmers are tired. A great streamline here is a distinct advantage.

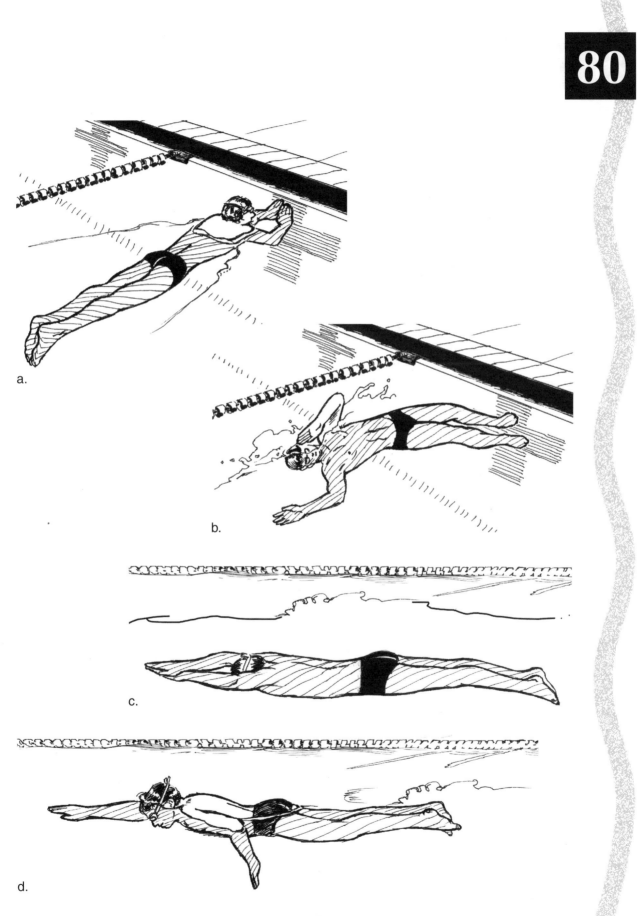

a.

b.

c.

d.

81

Freestyle Finish

Purpose

To perform a proper freestyle finish.

Description

The most common errors by swimmers include breathing inside of the last 5 yards, lifting the head prior to the finish, gliding into the wall, and finishing on top of the wall instead of into the wall or touch pad.

1. Start 10 to 12 yards away from the wall. Swim freestyle at full speed toward the wall.

2. Keep your eyes focused forward. Control your breathing at least from the time you pass the flags to the wall.

3. On the last stroke, extend and reach for the wall with one hand touching it underwater. Don't stop kicking. Your fingertips should touch first. Keep your eyes underwater so that you can see your hand touch the wall.

Focus Points

- Control your breathing.
- Kick aggressively.
- Touch underwater.
- Watch your hand touch.

Tip

If you focus on your competitors during the finish, you lose focus on your own finish. Stay focused on the wall.

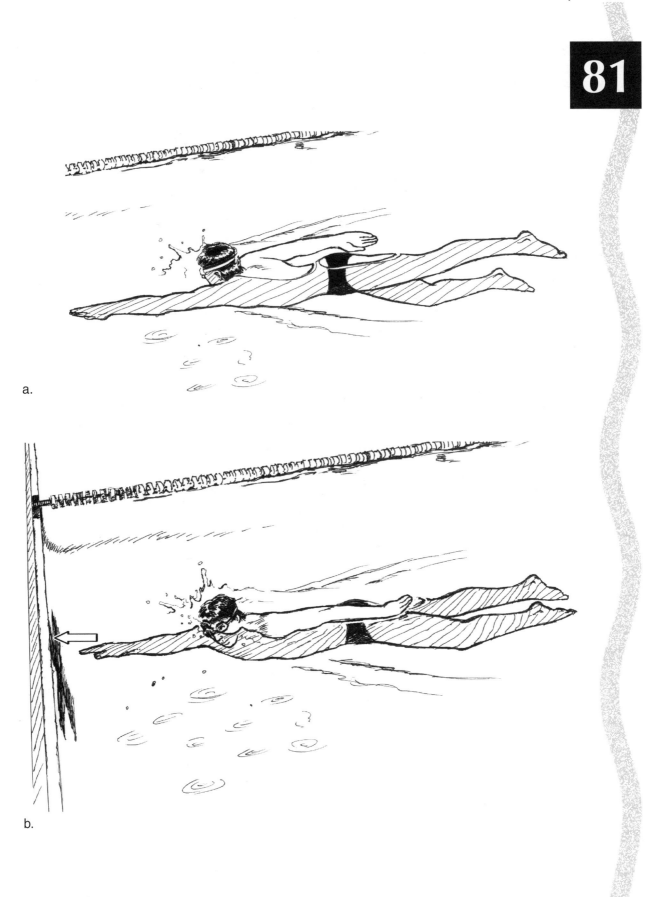

a.

b.

Jeff Rouse in the 100 meter backstroke, 1994. © Dan Helms

CHAPTER NINE

Starts

"Swimmers, take your mark. . . ."

Then the gun or horn sounds! Watching a swimmer with a great start is like watching a true act of beauty: quick release, tremendous launch through the air, smooth entry, tight streamline, and rapid travel through a great distance underwater, then coming up well ahead of the pack. If performed well, the start can make a significant difference in the outcome, especially in the sprint races. Conversely, a poor start can leave a swimmer well behind.

These drills concentrate on

- developing leg strength and power;
- discovering your balance point when starting from the blocks; and
- attaining a tight streamline position and controlling the depth of your dive.

The drills in this chapter help swimmers make stronger and faster starts. All of these drills are a lot of fun as well. Swimmers seem to always like practicing starts!

Backstroke Start

Purpose

To perform a proper backstroke start.

Description

Focus on getting your hips up high above the water as you leave the wall.

1. To set up for the backstroke start, hold onto the gutter. Place your feet on the wall about shoulder-width apart, approximately 2 feet deep.

2. Keep your hips out, away from the wall; do not tuck them in toward the wall.

3. When the referee says "Take your mark," bend your elbows and bring your nose in toward your hands, but keep your hips out.

4. On "Go," release your hands, throw your head back, and spring off the wall.

5. To learn to arch your back properly, practice in shallow water (4 to 5 feet). From the wall, push off and immediately perform a back dive into a handstand position. Try to hit the handstand just a few feet away from the wall.

6. Next, have someone hold a kickboard or a soft floating tube at the surface about 3 to 5 feet from the wall (depending on your size). Try to dive backward over the board or tube without letting your hips touch it. Immediately reach a streamline position and complete a backstroke breakout.

7. Finally, remove the board or tube and perform the backstroke start. You want your hips to clear the water surface as you leave the wall. Then immediately get into a tight streamline position and control your depth as you complete the backstroke breakout.

Focus Points

- Set up properly. Keep your hips out, away from the wall.
- Arch your back so that your hips clear the surface.
- Get into a tight streamline right away.

Tip

Practice taking off from the wall with your hands holding the gutter handles before moving up to the handles on the blocks.

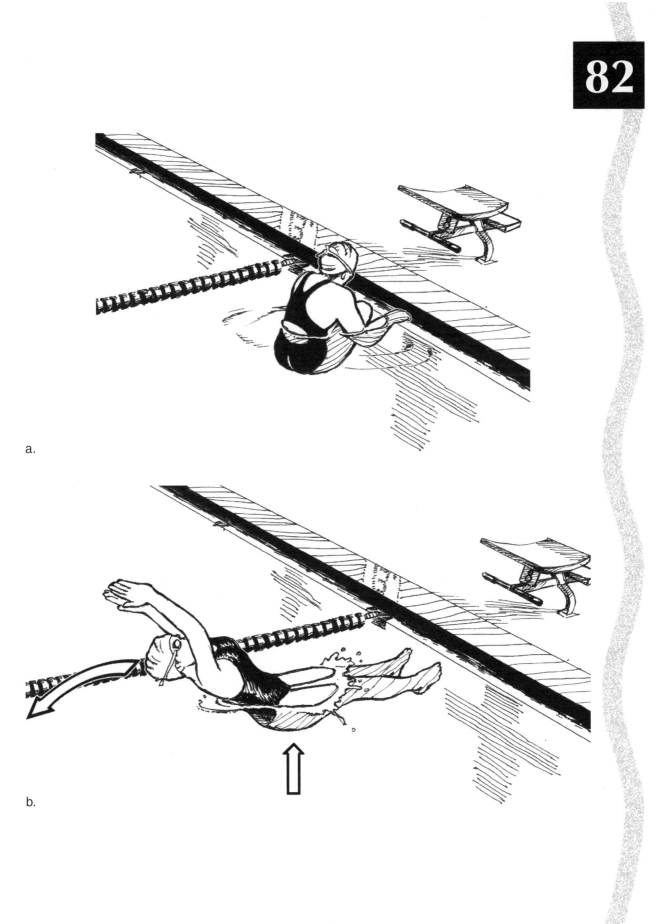

a.

b.

83

Jumping From the Deck

Purpose

This begins a series of drills to develop better starts from the blocks.

Description

1. Place your feet at the edge of the pool. It is usually better to have both feet forward instead of a track start (one foot forward, the other foot back) for this drill.

2. Bending your knees and using your arms to swing forward, jump from the deck into the pool and land feet first as far into the pool as you can.

3. Extend your feet as you leave the deck so that you spring off your toes.

Focus Points

- Keep your head forward.
- Get as much distance as possible. Use those legs.

Tip

Practice jumping rope and standing broad jumps to increase your leg strength and jumping ability.

a.

b.

Jumping From the Blocks

Purpose

The next step in this series of drills allows practice in jumping from the blocks.

Description

This is exactly the same as the previous drill, except you will now move up to the blocks.

Focus Points

- Keep your head forward.
- Get as much distance as possible by using your legs.

Tip

Have someone measure your distance. You should be able to jump farther from the blocks than from the deck.

a.

b.

Rolling Jump From the Blocks

Purpose

This next step helps swimmers discover their balance point when they are on the blocks. As a result, swimmers can "set" on the balance point more easily when they take their mark.

Description

1. On command, come down and take your mark on the blocks.
2. Slowly roll forward until you can no longer keep your body on the blocks.
3. Then release forward and jump.
4. Try to determine where your most forward balance point is when you are on the blocks.

Focus Points

- Slowly roll forward past your balance point.
- Feel where the balance point is for you.

Tip

Try to pause just a little at the balance point before rolling forward.

a.

b.

c.

86

Pushoff Start From the Wall

Purpose

This drill is designed to teach the mechanics of the release and body entry. If done properly, it is just like a butterfly entry.

Description

1. Position yourself in the water facing away from the wall, with your hands behind you holding the gutter wall and your feet up high on the wall.

2. Lunge forward and slightly above the surface as you release from the wall. Your arms will travel forward just like a butterfly recovery.

3. As your hands come forward and together, get your forehead down and dive into the water, just as you would for the butterfly.

4. Immediately reach a tight streamline position. You should have a clean entry.

5. If you time it right, you will be able to perform a small dolphin kick as your feet enter the water.

Focus Points

- Get your head down quickly as you enter the water.
- Punch a clean hole into the water as you enter.
- Get into a tight streamline right away.

Tip

Try diving over a loose lane rope or some other soft obstacle.

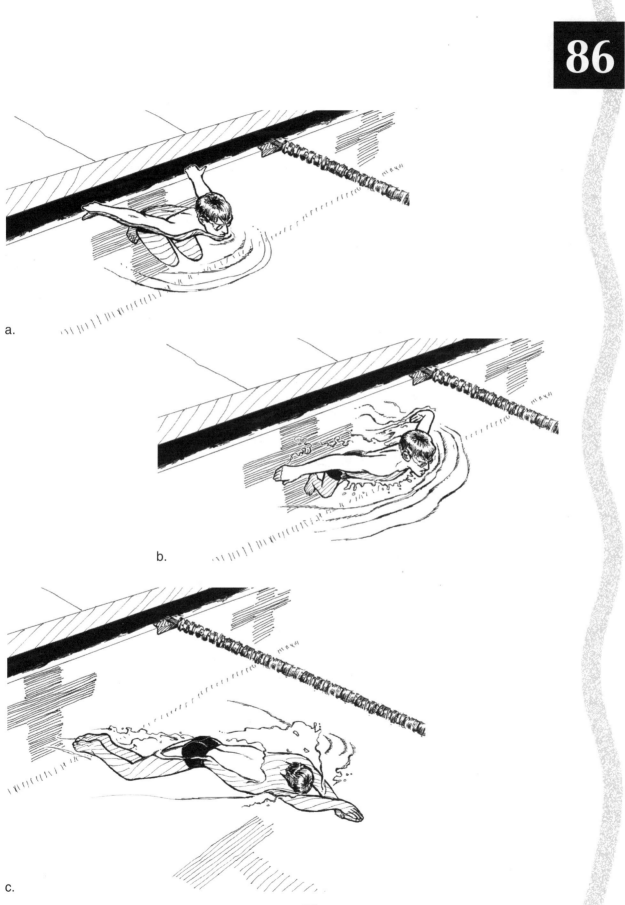

a.

b.

c.

Dive From the Deck

Purpose

This next step in the series will teach the dive from the deck. Use the same mechanics from the two previous drills.

Description

1. Stand on the edge of the deck and come down to take your mark.
2. Roll forward slowly until you can no longer stay on the deck.
3. Then release and dive forward by extending over the water, recovering your arms as in the butterfly, and reaching a tight streamline position as you enter the water.
4. Try to punch a clean entry into the water.

Focus Points

- Roll forward, then release.
- Reach the streamline as you enter the water.
- Punch a clean entry.

Tip

Practice diving over a soft obstacle or through a hula hoop on the surface of the water.

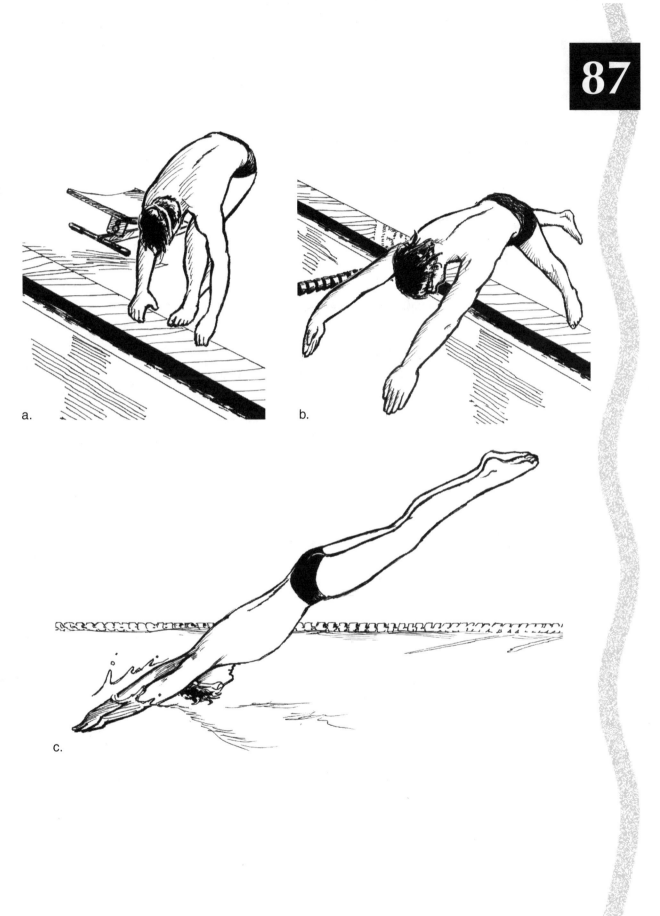

a.

b.

c.

88

Dive From the Blocks

Purpose

The final step for learning how to dive from the blocks.

Description

The action of this drill is exactly the same as the previous drill, except that you will now launch from the blocks.

1. Stand on the edge of the blocks and come down to take your mark.

2. Roll forward slowly until you can no longer stay on the blocks.

3. Then release and dive forward by extending over the water.

4. Recover your arms as in the butterfly and reach a tight streamline position as you enter the water. Try to punch a clean entry into the water.

Focus Points

- Roll forward, then release.
- Reach the streamline as you enter the water.
- Punch a clean entry.

Tip

Practice diving over a soft obstacle or through a hula hoop on the surface.

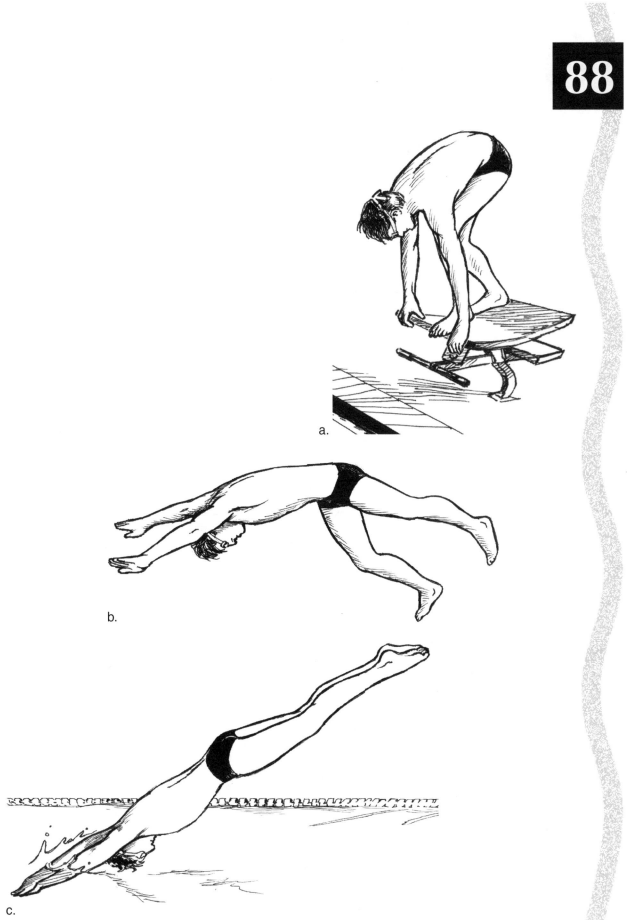

a.

b.

c.

89

Butterfly Start

Purpose

To add the butterfly breakout to the dive and entry.

Description

This will be a medium-depth entry.

1. Come down and take your mark. This time hold steady at the balance point.

2. On the command "Go," release and enter the water.

3. Once you enter the water, begin your butterfly breakout with the dolphin kicking.

4. Come to the surface and swim two to three strokes without breathing.

Focus Points

- Aim for a tight streamline on entry.
- Control your breathing for the first two to three strokes.

Tip

Do a dolphin kick as you enter the water.

89

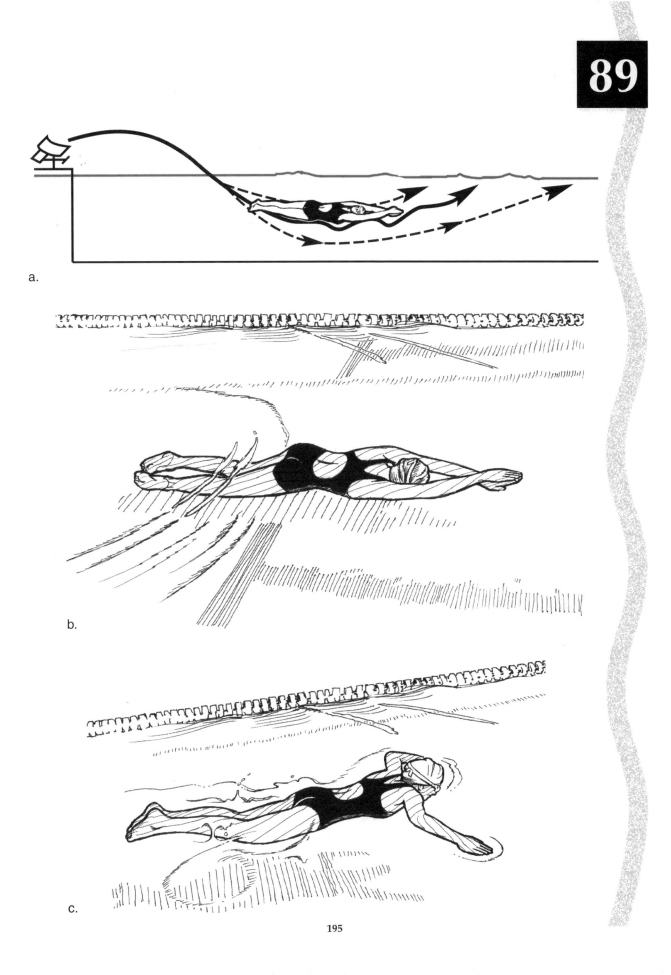

a.

b.

c.

90

Breaststroke Start

Purpose

To add the breaststroke pullout to the dive and entry.

Description

This will be the deepest of the dives. Generally, most swimmers should reach a depth of about 3 feet.

1. Come down and take your mark. Hold steady at the balance point.
2. On the command "Go," release and enter the water.
3. Once you enter the water, begin your breaststroke pullout by holding the streamline for a count of three.
4. Pull down and hold for a count of two.
5. Then kick up and stretch for a count of one before starting the breaststroke.

Focus Points

- Aim for a tight streamline on entry.
- Control the gliding for the pullout. Be patient.

Tip

See how far you can go underwater until you break the surface. Then have someone time how fast you can get to the same point on repeated efforts.

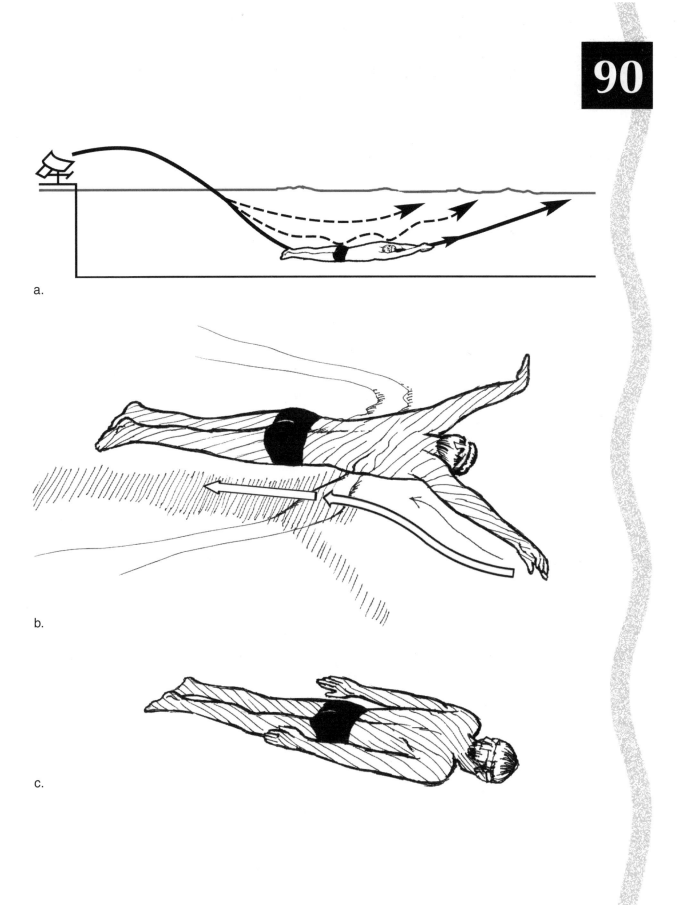

a.

b.

c.

91

Freestyle Start

Purpose

To add the freestyle breakout to the dive and entry.

Description

This will be the shallowest of the dives. Swimmers should reach the surface fairly quickly once they are in the water, especially on the shorter sprint races.

1. Come down and take your mark. Hold steady at the balance point.
2. On the command "Go," release and enter the water.
3. Once you enter the water, begin to kick quickly in a tight streamline position. Bring your head up fairly quickly.
4. Begin the freestyle by pulling down with one arm and breaking the surface.
5. Control your breathing for at least the first four strokes.

Focus Points

- Aim for a tight streamline entry.
- Kick very quickly.
- Come up to the surface quickly.
- Control your breathing.

Tip

Do a dolphin kick as you enter the water.

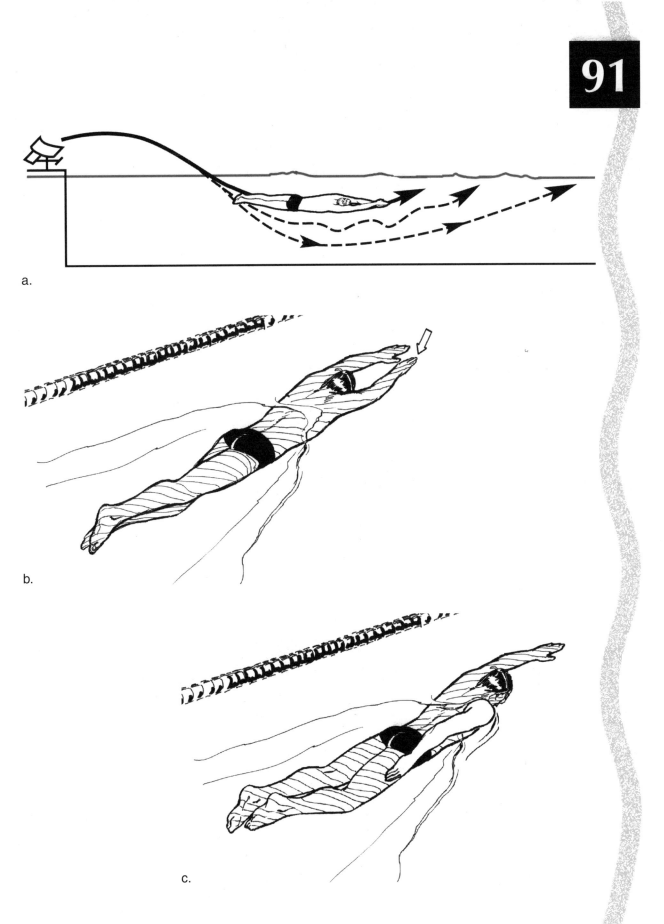

a.

b.

c.

ABOUT THE AUTHOR

Ruben Guzman, a United States Swimming (USS) coach for age-group swimmers, has coached swimming for more than 18 years at the summer recreational, high school, collegiate, and competitive year-round (USS) levels.

An expert on the mechanisms of the human body, Guzman has trained in physics, kinesiology, anatomy, education, and behavioral changes. He has a master's degree in Public Health and is also a health promotion specialist.

Some of Guzman's swimmers have advanced all the way to nationals and the Olympic trials. Having served as the "stroke specialist" for the California Capital Aquatics team, Guzman has worked closely with head coach Mike Hastings, an assistant coach on the 1992 United States Olympic Team.

Guzman recently founded a new USS team, the American River Gold, centered in Sacramento, California, where he currently lives. When he's not coaching or swimming, he enjoys playing basketball, snow skiing, and other activities with his two sons.

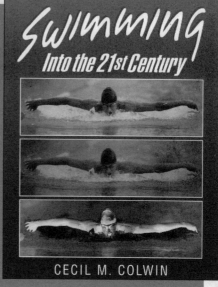